Hamsters

Hamsters

Project Team
Editor: Stephanie Fornino and Heather Russell-Revesz
Technical Editor: Tom Mazorlig
Interior Design: Leah Lococo Ltd. and Stephanie Krautheim
Design Layout: Angela Stanford

T.F.H. Publications
President/CEO: Glen S. Axelrod
Executive Vice President: Mark E. Johnson
Publisher: Christopher T. Reggio
Production Manager: Kathy Bontz

T.F.H. Publications, Inc.
One TFH Plaza
Third and Union Avenues
Neptune City, NJ 07753

Discovery Communications, Inc.
Book Development Team:
Marjorie Kaplan, President, Animal Planet Media
Carol LeBlanc, Vice President, Licensing
Elizabeth Bakacs, Vice President, Creative Services
Brigid Ferraro, Director, Licensing
Peggy Ang, Director, Animal Planet Marketing
Caitlin Erb, Licensing Specialist

Printed and bound in China
09 10 11 12 13   5 7 9 8 6

Library of Congress Cataloging-in-Publication Data
Fox, Sue, 1962-
  Hamsters / Sue Fox.
    p. cm. – (Animal Planet pet care library)
  Includes bibliographical references.
  ISBN 0-7938-3768-5 (alk. paper)
  1. Hamsters as pets. I. Title. II. Series.
  SF459.H3F69 2006
  636.935'6–dc22
  2006007719

This book has been published with the intent to provide accurate and authoritative information in regard to the subject matter within. While every reasonable precaution has been taken in preparation of this book, the author and publisher expressly disclaim responsibility for any errors, omissions, or adverse effects arising from the use or application of the information contained herein. The techniques and suggestions are used at the reader's discretion and are not to be considered a substitute for veterinary care. If you suspect a medical problem consult your veterinarian.

The Leader in Responsible Animal Care for Over 50 Years!®

www.tfh.com

CENTRAL
Garden & Pet

Table of Contents

Chapter 1

Why I Adore My
Hamster

Hamsters are among the most popular small animal pets in the world, especially for children. In fact, the hamster's charming looks and amusing antics intrigue children, and caring for a pet such as this is often a rite of childhood.

If you have never kept a pet hamster, you undoubtedly have expectations as to what doing so will be like. The best way to have a good experience is to know as much as you can about hamsters before sharing your home with one. Knowing ahead of time how this animal interacts with people and the type of care he needs will help you determine if he can meet your expectations and whether you can properly care for him.

As with any pet, the decision to buy a hamster should not be made on impulse. Choosing the right pet requires careful thought and some research. The information in this book will help you make a good choice by answering questions on how well a hamster might fit into your family.

There are four species of dwarf hamster.

Hamster History

Today, five species of hamster are found as laboratory animals and pets all over the world. These include four species of dwarf hamster, as well as the Syrian, or golden, hamster (*Mesocricetus auratus*). How these species came to be popular pets is an interesting story.

Unlike colorful Amazon parrots and singing canaries, hamsters did not originally enter the realm of domestication as pets. They were first coveted by medical researchers in China during the early 1920s, when it was discovered that the Chinese hamster (*Cricetulus griseus*) was very susceptible to infection with *Leishmania donovani*, the protozoan organism that causes kala-azar. This disease afflicts people in India, China, Russia, Africa, the Mediterranean basin, and several South and Central American countries. The Chinese hamster became the first satisfactory laboratory animal for the study of leishmaniasis.

Researchers paid farmers for each hamster they dug up in their grain fields. The supply was ample, and thousands were used to study the disease. The hamsters were kept in isolated cages, because if they were placed together, fights to the death occurred. Numerous attempts by early researchers to breed the Chinese hamster failed due to the hamsters' pugnacious habits whenever adults were paired.

The Syrian Hamster

Researchers were eager to get any rodent of the hamster group for their research on leishmaniasis. The Syrian, or golden, hamster was considered only after the Armenian hamsters (*Cricetulus migratorius*) and Chinese hamsters failed to breed in captivity. In 1930, a naturalist in Syria dug up a burrow containing a mother hamster and her litter for a researcher at Hebrew University in Jerusalem. The Syrian hamster then rose to worldwide prominence because they readily bred in captivity. Within a year, these prolific animals had produced more than 300 Syrian hamsters in the first laboratory colony.

Until 1971, all hamsters were descendents of the first animals captured in 1930. In 1971, though, a researcher caught 13 Syrian hamsters in Aleppo, Syria, and brought them to the United States, where they contributed to the gene pool of laboratory and pet hamsters. Considering how inbred Syrian hamsters are, relatively few serious problems related to low genetic diversity are noted among them.

Dwarf Hamsters

By the 1950s, four species of dwarf hamsters were also successfully reared in captivity.

In fact, dwarf hamsters are adorable little animals who have been kept as pets for more than 30 years. Dwarf hamsters are not just miniatures of the commonly kept golden or Syrian hamster. They are several distinct species with different looks, habits, and pet qualities. The four species of dwarf hamsters kept as pets are:

- Campbell's Russian hamster (*Phodopus campbelli*)
- Winter White hamster (*Phodopus sungorus*)
- Roborovskii's hamster (*Phodopus roborovskii*)
- Chinese hamster (*Cricetulus griseus*)

7

The Syrian hamster rose to worldwide prominence because he readily bred in captivity.

The Syrian hamster is also known as the teddy bear hamster.

Understanding Taxonomy

You will notice that each hamster is referred to by a common name, such as Campbell's Russian hamster, and by a scientific name, *Phodopus campbelli*, which is italicized and follows in parenthesis. Scientific names and classifications can seem complex and boring. However, in the case of dwarf hamsters, this information is very important.

Taxonomic Categories

Taxonomic categories are scientists' method for ordering all living things. The taxonomic groups are the following: kingdom, phylum, class, order, family, genus, and species name. A species is the basic unit of classification, such as Campbell's Russian hamster (*P.*

campbelli). Generally, a species is made up of organisms morphologically similar and able to breed among themselves but not able to breed with members of another species. Genera (singular is genus) are groups of species that share a common ancestor. Genera are grouped into families, families into orders, orders into classes, classes into phyla, and phyla into kingdoms. Thus, the Campbell's dwarf hamster belongs to the kingdom Animal; phylum Chordata; class Mammalia; order Rodentia; family Muridae; genus *Phodopus*; and species *campbelli*. When reading further about dwarf hamsters, always check the scientific name to be sure the writer is referring to the same species in which you are interested.

The Chinese hamster has a silky coat.

Roborovskii's Hamster

Other Common Names: desert hamster

Description: 2 inches (5.1 cm) in length, sandy brown with a white belly. White marks above their eyes look like eyebrows, and white whiskers on their snout make them look unshaven.

Country of Origin: Mongolia, China, Russia

Chinese-Striped Hamster

Other Common Names: striped hamster, rat-like hamster

Description: 4 to 5 inches (10.2 to 12.7 cm) in length, grayish-brown with a black dorsal stripe. Juveniles are sometimes grayer than adults. The fur feels silky.

Country of Origin: China

Winter White Hamster

Other Common Names: Siberian hamster, striped hairy-footed hamster, Winter White Russian hamster

Description: About 4 inches (10.2 cm) in length, gray color with a white belly. As the days become shorter in fall and winter (less than 8 hours of light each day), the gray coat molts into solid white. The white color helps to camouflage the hamster against the snow and protect him from potential predators.

Country of Origin: Mongolia, Manchuria, Siberia, and sections of China.

Note: At one time, the Campbell's Russian hamster and the Winter White hamster were considered the same species, but later, researchers showed they were distinct species. Some hobbyists have bred the two species together, and the resulting hybrid offspring are often infertile.

Syrian Hamster

Other Common Names: golden hamster, teddy bear hamster

Description: 5 to 7 inches (12.7 to 17.8 cm) in length, wild color is golden brown with black cheek flashes and white feet.

Country of Origin: Aleppo in northwestern Syria

Campbell's Russian Hamster

Other Common Names: Djungarian hamster, striped hamster, hairy-footed hamster

Description: 3 to 4 inches (7.6 to 10.2 cm) in length, gray-brown color, white belly, thick, woolly-feeling coat

Country of Origin: Northern China, Mongolia, central Asia, southern Siberia

> *The only way to know for certain which species you are talking about is by the scientific name.*

hairy-footed hamster, Siberian hamster, and Djungarian hamster), but its scientific name, *Phodopus campbelli*, is always the same. In addition, its first two common names are also used for another species of hamster, the Winter White hamster (*P. sungorus*). Without the scientific name, the common name "Siberian hamster" can mean either the Campbell's Russian hamster (*P. campbelli*) or Winter White hamster (*P. sungorus*).

Scientific Names

Scientific names are the means by which scientists and pet owners from all over the world refer to the same species of animal. The only way to know for certain which species you are talking about is by the scientific name. A species' scientific name is made of two parts: the genus and the species epithet. The first letter of the genus name is always capitalized. If

Common Names

Scientists and professional hobbyists use scientific names because an animal can have several different common names. Common names can vary by region and can even be the same as another animal's common name. The dwarf hamster species are a good example of the confusion that can arise from common names. For example, Campbell's Russian hamster is known by at least three other common names (striped

The word "hamster" comes from the German verb "hamstern," which means "to hoard."

the genus was previously written in full, it can also be denoted by the first letter followed by a period. The genus and species name is always italicized or underlined.

All dwarf hamsters belong to the genus *Phodopus*, which roughly translates to "blister foot" and refers to the large joined pad on the sole of each foot. The Chinese hamsters belong to the genus *Cricetulus* and are referred to as rat-like hamsters because their long faces, thin bodies, and long tails make them look somewhat similar to a rat. Hamster hobbyists call all the small hamster species dwarf hamsters. The other three hamster genera are mouse-like hamsters, genus *Calomyscus*, the common or black-bellied hamster, *Cricetus,* and the Syrian, or golden, hamster, *Mesocricetus*.

About Hamsters
Twenty-four 24 species of hamsters exist, but as mentioned earlier, only five species are kept as pets. These animals are found in Europe, the Middle East, Russia, and China. Most species live in arid, desert-like habitats.

Size
Hamsters are small, between 2 and 4 inches (5.1 to 10.2 cm) in length, with tiny tails that are barely visible. However, hamsters in the genus *Cricetulus*, including the Chinese hamster, have longer tails.

Habitat
Hamsters live in long underground burrows that they dig with their sharp

claws. They dig separate chambers for sleeping, storing food, and pottying. Their long whiskers help them navigate underground as well as above ground.

Feeding Habits
The word "hamster" comes from the German verb *hamstern*, which means "to hoard." These animals have expandable cheek pouches that are lined with fur. They use their

The Hamster's Life Span

Most species of hamsters have a short life span, typically between 1.5 to 2 years of age. However, the Chinese and Roborovskii's dwarf hamsters can live up to 3 years. A short life span can be unfortunate for pet owners who become attached to their hamsters. However, one advantage of the short life span is that hamsters do not live so long that children become disinterested in them. For example, long-lived pets, such as rabbits, can become neglected by children as they mature and become interested in other activities.

All dwarf hamsters belong to the genus Phodopus, *which roughly translates to "blister foot."*

pouches to carry food and bedding back to their burrows. Food is usually collected in one pouch at a time. When enough desirable food is available, a hamster will fill his pouches to the bursting point. These full pouches extend past the hamster's shoulders and make him look misshapen. In fact, when full of food, the pouches more than double the width of a hamster's head and shoulders. Hamsters use their front paws to fill their pouches, as well as to squeeze the food out of the pouches.

Hamsters are able to carry, and thus store, great quantities of food in their underground storage chambers. This adaptation allows them to survive on stored food when food is scarce. In Europe, a wild common hamster

(*Cricetus cricetus*) was found with almost 200 pounds (90.7 kg) of food in his pantry! During famines in China, peasants survived by digging up the giant hamsters' (*C. triton*) buried grain stores. (Hamsters spend the winter in hibernation in their burrows, only waking on warmer days to eat food from their pantry.)

Hamsters have powerful jaw muscles and teeth and can easily gnaw through a variety of substances, including plastic and wood. They have two pairs of chisel-like incisors in the front of their mouths, enabling them to easily open hard seeds, grains, and nuts. Although these incisors never stop growing, they are constantly worn down when the hamster gnaws and chews on hard substances. If you look at a hamster's front teeth, you will notice that the lower incisors are longer than the upper incisors. His molars, on the other hand, do not keep growing. Between a hamster's incisors and rear molars is a space called the "diastema." When he eats, his cheeks block this space to prevent any sharp food from being swallowed. Food enters the hamster's large cheek pouches from a hole in the diastema.

Sight, Hearing, and Smell

Hamsters have poor eyesight and can only judge distances a few inches (cm) in front of their face. However, they have an acute sense of hearing. Aside from the squeaks that people can hear, hamsters, unlike people, can also communicate and hear sounds in the ultrasonic range. Scientists believe that ultrasonic sounds are important during mating.

A keen sense of smell helps hamsters recognize other hamsters (as well as detect whether they are male or female), locate food, and

Gentle, regular handling will make most hamsters docile.

detect pheromones used in social interactions. In fact, hamsters communicate with one another through pheromones, which are chemicals secreted from the body that facilitate communication and influence behavior between members of the same species.

Both male and female Syrian hamsters have scent glands that they use to mark their territory. The most obvious glands are located on each hip, appearing slightly darker than the surrounding fur. Both sexes of dwarf hamsters also have a scent-producing gland in the middle of their bellies. It is not conspicuous, appearing like a small hairless patch that is larger in males than in females. While the smell from these glands is obvious to other hamsters, you are unlikely to ever notice it. Besides using their scent glands, hamsters also mark their territory with urine and droppings.

14

The Hamster as a Pet

Hamsters are inexpensive, undemanding, and easy to care for. In many ways, they make the perfect pet for both children and adults alike.

Aggressive Tendencies

Hamsters typically bite only when they are afraid or threatened. Gentle, regular handling will make most hamsters docile and reduce the likelihood of ever being bitten. With frequent handling and attention, most hamsters become tame and make good pets. It typically requires time, patience, and a food treat to win their trust, though.

Compared to Syrian hamsters, dwarfs are more easily awakened during the day, thus decreasing the likelihood that they will bite an unwary pet owner. Hamsters are sound sleepers and grouchy when awakened without warning. More important, if they do bite, dwarfs are less likely to break the skin. When you place your hand into a cage of dwarf hamsters, they will often run up to your hand to investigate.

At night, hamsters make many noises, gnawing, cracking seeds, drinking water, and running on their exercise wheels. While play-fighting with each other, you are likely to hear soft squeals and chatter.

Care Requirements

Unlike pets such as ferrets and rabbits, hamsters are low maintenance and do not require a great deal of daily attention, fitting in well with many peoples' busy lifestyles. Even if you are away from home during the day and early evening, a hamster will not have missed your companionship. He will just be waking up and getting ready to start his "day."

Because hamsters hoard food and do not drink large amounts of water, they can even tolerate some degree of occasional childhood neglect. Hamsters can remain unattended in their cage with extra food and water over a weekend. Because they don't require specialized care, they and their cage can easily be left with a friend or relative during family vacations. Even if they are not given much attention, tame hamsters seldom become withdrawn and easily frightened, whereas other small pets, such as rabbits, do withdraw.

Hamsters require routine feeding and cleaning, but they do not need lots of your time for playing outside their cage. They can be kept in their cage full time, as long as they are provided a spacious, entertaining, and toy-filled cage in which to play. A pair of dwarf

hamsters can be as interesting and relaxing to watch as an aquarium of tropical fish. These active little animals are constantly moving and exploring.

Cleanliness

A pet hamster is very clean, performing an elaborate grooming ritual several times a day. The hamster first licks his front feet, or hands. Then, using both hands, he washes his face and behind his ears. Using his hind foot, the hamster delicately cleans the inside of his ears and then nibbles clean his toes. He continues washing the fur all over his body and then licks his hind toes after scratching with them. In short,

The Expert Knows

Hamsters and the Law

In some states, certain species of pets are not legal for pet stores to sell or for you to own. Although national legislation governs the keeping of animals, individual states still have their own laws, and these laws vary from state to state, from county to county, and even from city to city. States can ban personal ownership of an animal species for various reasons. For example, in California, it is not legal to keep Chinese hamsters (Cricetulus griseus) as pets. The California Department of Fish and Game has banned this species because of concerns that if Chinese hamsters become established in the wild, they could damage crops and displace native wildlife. In general, if a hamster species is offered for sale in the pet stores within your state, it is probably legal for you to own.

hamsters are very fastidious, and most will even set up a separate toilet area in their cage.

Size

A hamster's small size appeals to both adults and children, who may become captivated by the animal's adorable, roly-poly appearance. However, hamsters are not cuddly pets. Tame hamsters do not mind being petted, but they also do not like being held for long periods. Although often referred to as pocket pets, young hamsters will not sit still for long in a pocket, and they will not ride on a person's shoulder like a pet rat will. In fact, their large black or red eyes make it seem like they should have good vision, but hamsters have poor depth perception and will tumble off a shoulder or fall from a table. Such falls can result in fatal injuries. In the wild, hamsters are ground-dwelling animals, and so they never needed to be able to judge their height above the ground.

Choosing a Pet Hamster

Choosing a pet hamster is an exciting decision that should nevertheless be approached carefully. You must consider many things, including the basic differences among the species; the best place to purchase your hamster; what variety, gender, age, and number of hamsters appeal to you most; and what kind of physical condition you should be looking for in a potential pet. This section will help you to determine all these things.

The Different Species

The best way to choose which species of hamster to purchase is to buy the one whose looks most appeal to you. The differences between the species are discussed below. Overall, some of these differences can be attributed to breeders who select for docile dispositions; other differences should be attributed to the fact that the species themselves are different.

Syrian Hamster (Golden Hamster)

This largest species of pet hamster is also the most common. While lively and active when young, they usually grow into calm pets. They are usually easier for children to handle, compared with dwarf hamsters, because they are larger and more robust. When

Before you choose your hamster, consider what variety, gender, and age appeal to you the most.

mouse, the Chinese hamster uses his short prehensile tail and paws to cling to his owner's fingers. Compared to the other dwarf hamsters, the Chinese is a relatively good climber and jumper. Photographs taken by European researchers in Peking, China, in 1930, show a street circus conducted by a man with Chinese hamsters trained to expertly perform acrobatics tricks in an elegant, hamster-sized big top complete with trapezes.

Roborovskii's Hamster
This smallest species of pet hamster is also the fastest and can move like greased lightening, so he must be held in cupped hands and continually walked between one's hands. In fact, because these hamsters are so small and fast, they are difficult for many pet owners to handle. If they escape while being held, they can be especially difficult to catch. This species can sometimes jump 1 foot (0.3 km) straight up in the air. Once tame, they become somewhat calmer, but Roborovskii's hamster is a very active animal. Because most children like to hold their pets, this is the least suitable dwarf species to consider for children.

Roborovskii's hamsters are fascinating pets to watch if housed in a large, entertaining cage. In some

full grown, they are less likely to bolt and leap out of your hands. Compared with dwarf hamsters, Syrians are more likely to hold still for some petting and cuddling. However, they are territorial and must be kept one to a cage.

Chinese Hamster
This species can be aggressive with each other. Young, untamed Chinese hamsters can be nervous, and adult hamsters who are not used to people can be difficult to tame. However, once tame, individuals tend to become calm and are easily handled. Like a

The dwarf hamster is the smallest species of pet hamster and also the fastest.

ways, Roborovskii's hamsters are good ornamental pets, better to watch than to handle. Untamed individuals of this species do not tend to bite as readily as do the other dwarf species. This species is the least common dwarf hamster pet.

Winter White and Campbell's Hamster

These two species are grouped together because they tend to behave similarly as pets. With consistent interactions, these species are relatively easy to tame. Once tame, they are friendly, confident, and curious. Many individuals seem to enjoy being petted. These species are also active and like to run and move about. Winter White and Campbell's hamsters can interbreed and produce hybrid offspring. However, in the wild, these species do not interbreed because they do not exist in the same area.

Male or Female?

Unless you want to breed hamsters, the gender should not matter, because no significant differences are noted in pet quality between males and females. Some pet owners think that male Syrian hamsters are calmer than females, but enough exceptions exist that this is not a useful generalization. Adult female Syrian hamsters are heavier than males, while adult male dwarf hamsters are typically slightly larger than females. Male hamsters tend to scent mark more than females, but the odor is not readily detected by people.

Male hamsters can be differentiated from females by the distance between

Hamsters as Pets for Children

Children are often captivated with hamsters and have their heart set on a owning one as a pet. However, young children can have unrealistic expectations of a pet and become upset when their hamster does not behave as desired. Children might dream of holding and cuddling their hamster, and photographs showing snuggling hamsters suggest that these animals also enjoy this activity. However, hamsters usually don't like being snuggled for very long and might protest by leaping blindly away or struggling to escape. If a hamster struggles while being held, some children tend to squeeze even harder instead of relaxing their hold. This rough handling can frighten a hamster and cause him to bite. The child might then drop or throw the animal, which can be fatal.

For these reasons, parents should expect to be the primary caretaker of a young child's hamster and must show their child how to properly interact with him. A parent can help reduce the risk of a bite by showing children how to properly hold their pet and instructing them on what to do should their pet begin to wiggle—for example, return the hamster to his cage. A parent might even need to help take the hamster out of his cage so that the child can visit with him. Children should be told to open the cage and let the hamster come to them, rather than trying to pull them out of their home. Young children occasionally tease their pets and so must be supervised while they are playing with them.

Children also do not have long attention spans. Once the novelty of owning a pet wears off, caring for him can become one more dreary chore. The opportunity to buy new toys for their pets helps children maintain their interest. Children like to save their allowance to buy toys for their animals, because it allows them to role play as the caretaker.

Because dwarf hamsters are so small, they do not make the best pets for young children. The larger Syrian hamsters are a better choice.

determine a hamster's gender by comparing it to the other hamsters in the cage. The pet store employee should also be able to help you determine the gender of your pets.

Be aware that a female might be pregnant if she was not separated soon enough from the males. Because of the possibility of a female being pregnant, try to buy your hamster from a pet store where the females are kept separate from the males.

Where to Buy

Syrian and dwarf hamsters can be bought at pet stores or from hobbyists who are members of hamster clubs. If possible, spend some time looking at the hamsters available from various pet stores and breeders. As previously stated, some lines of hamsters are more likely to nip. Handling them or watching a pet store employee or breeder do so will give you an idea of the animal's temperament. Hamsters who are bred in large numbers are sometimes less friendly than hamsters bred by hobbyists specifically selecting for a docile temperament.

Although you might find it surprising, hamsters are exhibited in shows just like dogs, cats, and horses. The hamsters are judged by experts who determine how closely the hamsters conform to the ideal standard for shape, appearance, and color or

their anus and their genital papilla, which is much greater in males than in females. An adult male's scrotum will also create a bulge near his rump, but this is less easily detected in younger hamsters. The female has two rows of four nipples, but these can be difficult to see. Blowing on the hamster's belly can part the hair enough to detect the nipples. You can more readily

markings for their variety. As a potential pet owner, you should try to determine whether the show hamster you are considering is docile and easy to handle. Hamsters who are nervous, timid, or try to bite are less likely to win awards. Hobbyists who show their hamsters usually breed hamsters who have won awards; thus, hamsters with undesirable

Handling the hamster will give you an idea of the animal's temperament.

temperaments are less likely to be bred. Because temperament has a hereditary component, show hamsters bred by hobbyists tend to have better pet qualities (for example, they are confident, not nervous) than are randomly obtained dwarf hamsters whose

Breeding Your Hamster

Syrian hamsters can first breed when they are only 45 days old. Between five to nine babies (called pups) are born 15 to 18 days later. Baby hamsters are born pink and hairless with their eyes closed. They are weaned when they are 20 to 25 days old. Depending on the species, dwarf hamsters usually become mature somewhat later, between 60 to 135 days old. Their gestation period ranges from 18 to 25 days. Female hamsters are well known for litter abandonment and cannibalism. These events are more likely to occur if the hamster is a first-time mother, if she is stressed or disturbed, or was provided inadequate nutrition.

If you decide to breed hamsters, you can expect your pets to have babies for the duration of the female's reproductive life, which is about 1.5 years. Although this can be fun and interesting, do consider whether you are able to find new homes for all the babies your pets will be making. Pet stores might be interested, but they might not always need hamsters when you are trying to find new homes for your weaned pets.

A qualified veterinarian can spay a female hamster or neuter a male hamster, which would eliminate the hamsters' ability to breed. Although altering rabbits and ferrets is a fairly common procedure, it is rarely performed on hamsters.

heredity is unknown. You can find hobbyists who breed hamsters in the advertisement section of pet magazines and on the Internet.

Varieties

All small animals kept in captivity eventually develop mutations from their normal color. In the wild, animals who are unusual in color are more noticeable to predators and often do not live long enough to reproduce. Hence, unusual colors are not typically found in wild populations. A conspicuous color is not a problem for pet animals, though, since people protect pets from potential predators. Hobbyists have increased the prevalence of color mutations by selectively breeding hamsters with desirable colors.

By learning about genetics and carefully keeping track of the results of certain pairings, breeders are able to develop new mutations in color, coat length, and texture. Breeders attempt to "fix" the desirable trait by line breeding (for example, breeding a father with a daughter or a brother to sister). Due to inbreeding, line breeding can sometimes cause problems such as a shorter life span, greater susceptibility to health problems, or reduced fertility. Should you ever choose to show hamsters, you will want to learn more about the inheritance of coat types and color. You could even try to develop a new color or coat variety yourself.

Similar to cat breeds, hamster varieties differ from one another in color, markings, coat textures, and sometimes temperament. Some hamster hobbyists believe that hamsters of a certain color or coat pattern are gentler and calmer when compared with other varieties. Although some individuals of a certain variety might have these desirable traits, unfortunately, currently too many exceptions exist to say with any degree of certainty that one variety of hamster makes a better pet than another.

Pet stores usually do not stock a wide variety of hamsters. If you want a particular color or a particular species of dwarf hamster that proves hard to find, ask whether a pet store can special-order the hamster for you from their suppliers. You can also contact the breeders listed on Internet sites that

The Syrian hamster has a long-haired variety.

Hamsters come in dozens of colors, including a spotted type.

are devoted to hamsters and their clubs.

The following are some common varieties available for the Syrian hamster, Campbell's Russian hamster, Chinese hamster, Roborovskii's hamster, and Winter White hamster.

Syrian Hamster

This species is available in one of four types of fur: normal, rex, satin, and long-haired. Normal fur is the most common and has two layers, an undercoat and an overcoat. Rex fur is short, stands upright, and feels like velvet. Satin fur is strikingly shiny and lustrous. The long-haired variety, also called angora or teddy bear, can have soft fur several inches (cm) long. This trait was first seen in the United Sates during the 1970s and, originally, only males had long coats. Although females are now readily available with long hair, many males still tend to have thicker, longer

coats than do females. Some long-haired hamsters need to have their coats brushed.

Syrian hamsters have been bred in dozens of colors, including black, cream, albino, gray, lilac, yellow, and cinnamon. They are also available in several patterns of color, but the three most common ones are tortoiseshell, banded, and dominant spotted.

Campbell's Russian Hamster
This species is available in more than two dozen different colors, including mottled black, lilac fawn, albino, champagne, black, argente (cinnamon- or sandy-colored), and blue, as well as their normal gray color. The eye color can be either black or red. This species can have the typical short-haired coat, or they can have a satin coat, which is very attractive, because the fur has a high, glossy sheen. Expect new colors and coat types to be developed in the future.

Chinese Hamster
The Chinese hamster is currently available in only two varieties. The normal color is dark gray-brown with a dark dorsal strip and off-white belly. The dominant spot is white with patches of color.

Roborovskii's Hamster
This species is currently available only in its natural sandy brown color.

Winter White Hamster
Currently, this species is available in only three colors. Besides the normal

If You Can't Keep Your Hamster

For various reasons, people sometimes can no longer keep their pet hamster. If you can no longer keep your pet, you should try to find him a new home by asking friends or your veterinarian if they know someone who wants a hamster. Also, try advertising in the newspaper. If that does not work, then you should relinquish your hamster with his cage and supplies to a humane society or shelter. Do not release your hamster into the wild in the mistaken belief that he will have a better chance at a happy life. Chances are he will be eaten by a predator or slowly die from an illness.

Young hamsters are much easier to tame.

gray color, look for pearl and sapphire. The pearl hamster is white with black eyes and is essentially the hamster's winter coat color. The sapphire is blue gray with black eyes. No coat differences have yet been developed.

Age

Pick a young hamster, because a young hamster is much easier to tame and will make a better pet than an older one who has been infrequently handled. Young hamsters will also live longer than an older animal. In particular, avoid buying an untamed adult Chinese hamster, as adults can be very difficult to tame.

Most species of hamsters are weaned between 3 to 4 weeks of age. They are ready to go to their new homes between 4 to 5 weeks of age. However, be sure not to buy a baby who was just weaned. Weaning, as well as going to a new home, are stressful events that can cause a baby hamster to get sick. A slightly older hamster will be hardier and just as cute. If the pet store employee does not know the age of the hamsters, you can estimate

their age by comparing their body length to their estimated adult size. (See sidebar for more information.)

Health

The premises of the pet store (or breeder) from which you buy your hamster should be clean, with minimal odor. Although some smell is normal, if the odor in the store or the hamsters' cage is excessively pungent, buy your hamster from another pet store. Also, check to be sure that the hamsters have food and water. An empty food dish or water bottle is a sign of poor care, and the hamsters are less likely to be healthy.

Choose your hamster from a clean, uncrowded cage. Hamsters who come from a dirty, crowded environment are less likely to be healthy. No matter how much you might like a particular hamster or want to purchase one on the spot, do not buy him if any of the hamsters in a cage exhibit symptoms of ill health. Although the hamster you want might appear healthy, he has been exposed to sick animals and is likely to become ill at a later time, often from the stress of going to a new home.

Hamsters should not limp or move awkwardly. A healthy hamster should have dense, shiny fur. The coat should be smooth and sleek, with no bald areas or flaky skin. In addition, the hamsters' eyes should be clear and bright. Your choice should look solid and a little plump. Do not choose a hamster who is listless, sneezes, has runny eyes or a runny nose, a rough or thin coat, lumps, or scabs. Dirty, matted fur near a hamster's tail could be a sign of diarrhea.

A healthy hamster is active and curious. Keep in mind that hamsters are nocturnal, so if you see them during the day, they are most likely going to be sleeping and will need to be awakened. This can take a while, because hamsters hate being awakened from their sleep. Ask the pet store employee to give them a handful of food, because this will sometimes cause them to become active. Also, try to shop for a hamster in the late afternoon or early evening, when they are more likely to be awake.

Personality

A hamster's temperament or personality is important to the quality of your pet-owning experience. Hamsters range in personality from calm and friendly to skittish and shy. Most pet owners enjoy calm hamsters better than they do a shy and skittish one. Personality is affected by hereditary factors and the environment in which an animal was reared. Few prospective pet owners are able to assess a hamster's family background, but the environment you provide and how often you play with him will affect his personality. By providing quality care and slowly taming your hamster, you are more likely to end up with an enjoyable pet.

You can increase the likelihood that you are buying a hamster with a good personality by choosing a hamster who

Hamsters	
Variety	**Adult Length**
Syrian Hamster	6 to 8 inches (15.2 to 20.3cm)
Campbell's Hamster	3.25 to 4.75 inches (8.3 to 12.1 cm)
Chinese Hamster	4 to 5 inches (10.2 to 12.7 cm)
Roborovskii's Hamster	1.5 to 2 inches (3.8 to 5.1 cm)
Winter White Hamster	2.25 to 4 inches (5.7 to 10.2 cm)

A healthy hamster should have dense, shiny fur.

is inquisitive and who investigates your hand when you place it in the cage. An animal who sniffs your hand and runs away but returns to further investigate your hand is a good choice. Just like puppies, some hamsters, in particular dwarfs, will explore their environment by nipping with their teeth. A nip from a dwarf hamster is not painful. It might startle you or frighten a child, but it will not draw blood. Do not choose a hamster who runs and hides, is aggressive and tries to bite, scratches, or struggles frantically when held.

A complicating factor in your selection is that many young hamsters enter an ornery, fearful stage in which they do not like to be held, even if they were previously handled. More unnerving is that some young Syrian hamsters rear up and scream when you try to pick them up. With gentle handling, they will outgrow this behavior.

How Many?

Syrian hamsters are solitary animals who must be kept in a cage by themselves. Once they are around 5 to 6 weeks of age, Syrian hamsters become territorial and will start to fight. You might wonder how pet stores can keep large numbers of Syrian hamsters in a group without them fighting. Often, they are littermates and, because they are constantly being sold and new individuals added to the group, fighting may be somewhat limited. Nonetheless, fights do happen, usually at night when no one is around.

Hamsters range in personality from calm and friendly to skittish and shy.

Settling Into a New Home

When you first bring your hamster home, he might be frightened and hide in his nest box. Some hamsters are more confident and will readily investigate their new home. Either way, let your new pet settle down and get used to his new home. Wait to show interested friends your new pet until after a few days have passed.

The first 3 weeks are the most stressful for hamsters as they adjust to a new environment. Talk to your hamster and think of a name for him, but do not try to hold him. You can eventually offer your new pet some of his food in your hand, but if he seems shy and nervous, leave him alone for a while, or talk soothingly to him. Sometimes partially covering all but the front of the cage with a brown paper bag will help your hamster feel more secure and less vulnerable. Once he becomes less nervous, you can completely remove the covering. Do not cover a wire cage with a towel, because your hamster will chew it.

A dwarf hamster can be kept by himself, or kept with others in small groups. Do not mix the different species of dwarf hamsters together, because they will aggressively fight and may even kill each other. Dwarf hamsters tend to be more active and playful when housed with others of their own kind. A hamster kept alone may be less active, and consequently, less interesting. If you want to keep more than one dwarf hamster, you must buy young hamsters (less than 8 weeks old) at the same time so that they can grow up together. The hamsters do not need to be littermates, but they should be approximately the same size to avoid bullying by the larger animal.

A group of dwarf hamsters will establish a dominance hierarchy. The dominant individuals are those who win fights and get the best food. Dwarf hamsters will play-fight with each other, but they will also fight to maintain

Choose a hamster who is inquisitive and who investigates your hand when you place it in the cage.

the dominance hierarchy. Loud squeaking can occur when hamsters are playing or fighting. Removing the higher-ranked or the lowest-ranked hamster will result in a shifting of the hierarchy but not necessarily a cessation of fighting. Unless a hamster is seriously injured, do not remove him. Once a hamster is removed from the group, it can be very difficult to reintroduce him back into the group—he is likely to be attacked.

Adult dwarf hamsters (about 8 weeks old) are territorial and will fight if another hamster is placed into their home. Dwarf hamsters who have been kept by themselves for most of their adult lives are not receptive to the introduction of another hamster. If one member of a pair dies, you can try to introduce another hamster. An adult hamster will more readily accept a younger hamster, but he might also attack the newcomer.

You can keep hamsters in single-sex or mixed-sex groups. Naturally, if you have more than one hamster, you must also buy a large enough cage and provide numerous nest boxes and other hiding places. Also, you need to keep in mind that if you keep a male and a female together, they will produce babies approximately every 20 to 36 days.

No matter what type of hamster you choose, whether it's the solitary Syrian who must be kept singly, or one of the dwarf species that can be kept in pairs, you are sure to enjoy keeping these charming little animals. Hamsters have been kept as pets for more than 50 years, and much is known about their habits and care. The information presented in the rest of this book will make caring for your hamster easy and enjoyable.

Dwarf hamsters tend to be more active and playful when housed with others of their own kind.

Chapter 2

The Stuff of
Everyday Life

Before you buy your hamster, you should purchase his cage and supplies and have everything ready prior to bringing home your new pet. If your pet's home is not yet set up, have someone else watch him while you arrange his new quarters, since a hamster can quickly chew out of the cardboard box provided by pet stores for the trip to your home.

lternatively, place the container in the bathtub so that your hamster cannot escape if he chews out of the box. Potential escapes are not a concern if you bring your pet home in a plastic small-animal carrier. However, do provide a dark, enclosed hiding container for your pet within his carrying cage. A hamster with no place to hide will feel exposed and stressed and can take longer to settle in.

The following are some basic supplies that you will need to make your new hamster's transition to your home easy and pleasant.

Bedding

Your hamster needs bedding in his cage. Bedding is used to absorb moisture (from urine and water from the occasional leaking bottle), reduce odors, and provide a warm, dry place for your pet to sleep. Bedding allows a hamster to engage in some natural behaviors, such as burrowing and building a sleeping nest.

Pet stores carry a variety of small-animal beddings that are suitable for hamsters, including wood shavings such as pine and aspen and more sophisticated beddings made from recycled paper or wood pulp that are designed to help control or eliminate odor. The latter types are more expensive, but they can make it more pleasurable to own hamsters, since their home is less likely to smell unpleasant between cage cleanings. Bedding made from recycled paper contains no harmful inks, dyes, or significant levels of heavy metals. Whatever bedding you choose, you only need a few inches. However, the bedding should completely cover the wire floor of a wire cage.

Bedding is an important component of your pet's environment,

Bedding allows a hamster to engage in some natural behaviors, such as burrowing and building a sleeping nest.

and it can affect his health. Ideally, small-animal bedding should be dust free. Dusty bedding can irritate a hamster's respiratory system or aggravate an existing respiratory ailment. Because hamsters live directly on their bedding, they are more likely to stir up fine particles and be at risk for these potential problems. In general, paper pulp and recycled paper products tend to be lower in dust compared to wood shavings.

The Shavings Controversy

Shavings made from softwoods, which include pine and cedar, are still the most common type of bedding for small pets. These beddings have been popular because they are relatively inexpensive and are often fragrant smelling, particularly cedar shavings. The pleasant smell associated with these materials is due to the aromatic compounds found in the wood. However, cedar shavings have been implicated as both causing and aggravating respiratory problems in small animals. In addition, they are known to affect liver function in rats and hamsters. However, few controlled, scientific studies have documented these problems. More common are reports that when a pet was removed from cedar shavings, its symptoms of poor health disappeared (such as sneezing). A few studies have shown that cedar shavings affect liver function in rats and mice, although the effect is so minute it is only of concern to

The Expert Knows

Activity Cycle

Syrian hamsters are nocturnal. They wake up in the early evening and usually are active until early in the morning. At night, your Syrian hamster will run about, eat his food, drink water, and make other noises. During the day, he will snooze soundly. Dwarf hamsters are primarily crepuscular, which means that they are most active in the early morning and early evening. They also sleep at night and during the day.

research scientists. While not all experts agree that cedar shavings pose a risk, it has become common practice to recommend against using them for small pets such as hamsters.

Some hobbyists also argue that pine shavings are harmful. However, no scientific evidence supports this assumption. Research facilities across the country still house small animals on pine shavings. If any detrimental effects occurred, scientists would be the first to switch beddings, because they cannot afford to have their research animals harmed. If you wish to avoid the issue completely, you can use shavings made from hardwoods such as aspen and spruce. However, they tend to be more expensive than pine and are not available everywhere.

The Stuff of Everyday Life

You can find bedding made from recycled paper.

Odor Control

The ammonia vapors from urine that develop in your pet's cage can make owning a hamster less pleasant. The harsh smell is also uncomfortable for the hamsters. Ammonia is a severe irritant and is detrimental to the health of these small animals. It affects the mucous membranes of their eyes and respiratory tracts. The health of hamsters with chronic respiratory conditions can worsen if they are regularly exposed to ammonia vapors, and the vapors can make them more susceptible to opportunistic infections. Hamsters housed on dirty, moist bedding are most susceptible to these effects, as are hamsters housed in aquariums that are infrequently cleaned.

The development of innovative bedding products has been spurred by the quest to control or eliminate odor. Scientifically developed bedding products made from a variety of materials, such as recycled paper, do not just mask odor—they are designed to reduce odor by controlling the formation of ammonia. Such beddings promote a healthier environment for hamsters compared with traditional wood shavings, and they are highly recommended. If your hamster is housed in an aquarium, if you are neglectful in cage cleaning, or if family members despise your pet because he smells, use innovative odor-controlling bedding.

Proper bedding will help control odor in your hamster's cage.

Move slowly, talk gently, and try to get close enough to offer him a sunflower seed. Alternatively, place his nest box close to where you saw him, trail some bedding and sunflower seeds into the entry, and your hamster might just dash for his "bedroom."

If these techniques do not work, place your pet's cage on the floor next to a wall, and leave the cage door open. You can leave a trail of sunflower seeds to the cage. You are likely to find your hamster back in his home the next morning. Naturally, if you have two hamsters, you cannot leave the cage door open, since the other hamster will join the wanderer. Instead, provide that hamster with a new nest box. Take the old nest box along with the nesting material and fresh food, and place it on the floor outside and next to the cage. Sometimes the hamster will return to the cage area and then fall asleep inside his familiar nest box.

If your hamster has decided that some secret location makes a better place to sleep and hoard sunflower seeds, then you will need to trap him. A variety of other methods can be used to attempt to catch an escaped hamster, including a ramp and empty bucket baited with food. Your pet will simply walk up the ramp and fall into the bucket.

The most effective and simple method to recapture your escaped pet is to use a harmless live trap baited with rolled oats and peanut butter. These traps are readily purchased at hardware stores or large chain stores. Place the live trap on the floor adjacent to a wall. Using more than one trap can increase your chances of quickly recapturing your pet. Buy traps made for mice, not the larger, rat-sized traps.

Despite all your precautions, your hamster might escape from his home or run away while you are playing with him. An escape is hazardous to your pet's health—he can starve to death or be eaten by other household pets such as dogs, cats, rats, and ferrets. An escaped hamster can also be very destructive, chewing on furniture, walls, and electrical wires. If your pet escapes outside, your chances of finding him alive again are not good.

Ideally, your hamster is still in your house, and you know which room he might be in. First, try to find your hamster by conducting a thorough search of every room. Once a room is cleared, place books along the door margin to prevent him from squeezing under the door. Have his nest box and some tasty treats, such as sunflower seeds, with you while you conduct your search. If you see your hamster, don't make any quick moves toward him, because doing so will frighten him and cause him to run away.

Exercise Wheel

An exercise wheel is mandatory for hamsters. Your pet can run for hours and will log several miles (km) on his wheel each night. Hamsters have been recorded running up to 8 miles (12.9 km) in one night on their wheel!

Exercise wheels come in a variety of styles and sizes. Free-standing wheels made of either plastic or metal are sold for use in aquariums or wire cages. Occasionally, dwarf hamsters have been known to get their small feet caught in wire-frame exercise wheels. Therefore, buy an exercise wheel with a solid floor for dwarfs. Such wheels are commonly sold in pet stores, or they can be special ordered. Dwarf hamsters can use an exercise wheel that is 5 to 6 inches (12.7 to 15.2 cm) in diameter.

Unlike dwarf hamsters, Syrian hamsters sometimes grow too large for their exercise wheel. If your pet has to arch his back while running on his wheel, he needs a larger one. Buy a wheel that measures at least 7 inches (17.8 cm) in diameter for your Syrian hamster. However, very large individuals might need a wheel as large as 9 inches (22.9 cm) in diameter.

Some exercise wheels develop an irritating squeak when the hamster runs on them. A small drop of vegetable oil can eliminate this problem.

Food Dish

Place your pet's food in a dish. If you have a metal cage, you can attach the dish to the side to prevent him from tipping it over and spilling the contents. If you use a free-standing dish, make sure it is heavy enough so that your hamster cannot tip it over. Pet stores sell a variety of colorful ceramic dishes that are too heavy for hamsters to move.

Using a dish can sometimes seem unnecessary, since your hamster will cart off favorite food items in his cheek pouches to store in his pantry. Nonetheless, placing the food in a dish

An exercise wheel is mandatory for hamsters.

instead of on the cage floor will prevent it from becoming accidentally contaminated with droppings and urine.

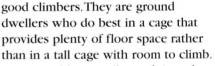

Housing

You can find a suitable cage for your hamster at a pet store. A cage is the most expensive piece of equipment you will need to acquire, and the general rule when buying a cage is that you should choose the largest that you can afford. At the very least, the cage you choose should be large enough to allow your pet room for separate eating, sleeping, and toilet areas, as well as one or two exercise wheels. No matter what species, hamsters are very active animals who need a roomy home. A cage that is too small and confining will become dirty and smelly more quickly, and it can lead to fights among your pets, because they will become irritable without enough space. The more room you provide your pets in which to play and explore, the more interesting and healthy they will be.

Types of Cages

Cages are available in many shapes, sizes, and styles. Hamsters are best housed in glass aquariums, wire-frame cages, or combination cages made of wire and plastic. Regardless of what style cage you choose, a few general rules apply. Hamsters are not arboreal (living in trees) and are not

good climbers. They are ground dwellers who do best in a cage that provides plenty of floor space rather than in a tall cage with room to climb.

Being able to easily reach into the cage to perform daily tasks such as cleaning and providing fresh food will help make these chores much easier. Whether a cage has both a top and front door or one large front door, at least one door should be large enough for you to comfortably reach all areas within the cage and be large enough for you to easily remove a hamster in your hand. Each door should latch securely and not be easily pushed out at a corner by a persistent hamster. No matter what type of housing you buy, immediately replace any part of your hamster's cage that is chewed or damaged, because it will not take long for him to find the damaged area and escape.

Aquarium-Style Cages

A 10-gallon (37.9-L) glass aquarium with a secure wire-screen cover will provide a good home for a single Syrian hamster or for a pair of dwarf hamsters. Because resourceful hamsters can always find a way out, their cage must always be covered. Pet stores sell wire screens just for this purpose, with latches to secure the top to the aquarium. The latches are a necessity, because hamsters can push a screen up just enough to slip out beneath it. Books and bricks placed on top of the cage as extra weight might be necessary, but extra latches are probably more secure.

Because the entire top lifts off the aquarium cage, you can readily reach your pet. Compared to a wire-frame cage, an aquarium will keep the area around your pet's home tidy, since shavings and other debris cannot spill out of the cage. However, the glass sides can become dirty and difficult to see through if they are not kept clean.

If you choose a glass aquarium or plastic small animal habitat, keep in mind that these types of housing are not as well-ventilated as a wire cage. Although these cages are beneficial because they are not drafty, poor ventilation and lax cleaning habits can cause ammonia gas to build up to uncomfortable levels. This can irritate your hamster's respiratory system. For your pet's health, you must be vigilant in keeping such a cage clean. If you can smell his home, then it is certainly an unhealthy environment for him, especially because he is right on top of the smelly bedding. If you think you might be neglectful in cage cleaning chores, select a wire-frame cage instead.

Finally, keep in mind that aquariums are heavier than wire cages and can be more difficult for a child to move and clean.

Wire-Frame Cages

A wire cage that measures 24 inches long by 12 inches wide by 10 inches high (61.0 cm by 30.5 cm by 25.4 cm) will provide a good home

An aquarium-style cage will keep the area around your pet's home tidy, since shavings and other debris cannot spill out.

Wire-frame cages made of galvanized steel have good ventilation and offer a good view of your pets.

cage should be easy to clean, with a slide-out or snap-off bottom tray.

Hamsters like to climb the bars of wire cages and use the top wires like monkey bars. The cage should have a large door opening that allows you to easily reach inside and take your hamster out. Check that the door latches securely and cannot be easily pushed out at a corner by your pet's super-hamster strength. Also, be sure that the cage has no sharp metal edges on the door. The best cages will have both a door and a removable top or side to provide easy access to the interior of the cage. A cage handle can make

for a single Syrian hamster or for a pair of dwarf hamsters. Wire-frame cages made of galvanized steel have good ventilation and offer a good view of your pets. The plastic trays of some cages are attractively colored and can be color coordinated to match a room's décor. A good quality wire-frame

The Escaping Hamster

Hamsters are noted for their ability to escape from their homes, often because someone forgets to securely close the cage door or because the hamsters chewed their way out of their enclosure. Both situations occurred to the zoology professor who collected the first group of Syrian hamsters in 1930. His original ten hamsters disappeared when the cage door was not properly closed. Four of them were quickly recaptured, but five of the escapees were only caught after great effort, worry, and several sleepless nights. The tenth hamster was never found.

When the nine hamsters were moved to Hebrew University, the animal caretaker housed them in a cage with steel screening and a wood floor. The hamsters' strong, sharp teeth and powerful jaw muscles quickly enabled them to gnaw through the thick wooden plank their very first night. Five hamsters escaped and were never found again. Of the four remaining hamsters, one was a female whose offspring gave rise to the majority of captive Syrian hamsters.

moving the cage easier. No matter the design, the wire mesh that comprises the body of the cage should feel strong and durable, not soft and flimsy.

Most manufacturers label their cages for specific kinds of small pets, such as for rabbits or hamsters. By choosing a cage designed for hamsters, you can assume that the size of the wire, called the *gauge*, is suitable, and that the spaces between the wire mesh are not so large that a Syrian hamster can squeeze out. However, wire cages do present a problem for owners of dwarf hamsters. Due to their small size, dwarf hamsters, especially young ones, can readily squeeze between the vertical bars of many rodent cages, even cages with bars that are only .5-inch (1.3-cm) apart. If your hamster can squeeze his head between the cage bars, the rest of his body will follow. For this reason, only choose a wire cage constructed with hatched wire mesh for your dwarf hamster. These are typically sold for mice. A potential drawback to a mouse cage is that mice do not need as much room as dwarf hamsters, and it can be difficult to find a mouse cage large enough for a dwarf hamster.

If you buy a wire cage with vertical bars that measure more than .25-inch (0.6-cm) apart, then you should also attach a heavy gauge wire mesh (not window screen!) that measures no greater than .25-inch (0.6-cm) square to the outside of the cage using metal clips. Do not use plastic ties, lightweight wire, or string to attach the additional wire mesh. These materials are not durable enough to withstand a dwarf hamster's chewing. The wire mesh should attach tightly to the original bars to prevent a hamster from squeezing between the two layers of wire and accidentally getting stuck.

Metal cages do have some other drawbacks. Although wire cages provide good ventilation, they are also potentially drafty. Also, over time, a hamster's relatively concentrated urine can corrode the metal pan that fits beneath a wire cage. You can help prevent this problem by cleaning your pet's bathroom area every few days or by lining the tray bottom with newspaper (as long as your hamster does not have access to the tray). Plastic trays will not corrode from urine, but many hamsters will chew on the plastic. Some hamsters

The cage can quickly become smelly if not cleaned frequently enough.

even climb the cage bars and mark the area outside their cage with urine.

Hamsters have tiny feet that can accidentally become caught and twisted in the wire floor of a metal cage. If the cage you choose has a wire rather than a solid floor, you must be certain to completely cover the floor with bedding to prevent this potential problem. Doing so will also prevent your hamster's food stores from dropping through the wire screen where he cannot reach them.

If you choose a wire-frame cage, try to find one with high bottom tray sides to catch bedding and other debris that your hamster will kick out during his normal activities. Alternatively, place the cage on top of newspaper that extends for several inches (cm) more than the cage's diameter, or place the cage inside a kitty litter pan to catch the material that spills out. You can also purchase a cloth seed guard sold in the bird section of a pet store.

Combination Wire and Plastic Cages

Combination cages constructed of wire screen and hard plastic are made just

for hamsters. These brightly colored cages are a lot of fun, because the connecting tubes allow you to expand your hamster's cage into a playground. Some dwarf hamsters have a difficult time crawling up vertical tubes, but placing the tubes horizontally between the cage units can make it easier for dwarf hamsters to move about.

Be picky with this type of housing, as some models can provide even less ventilation than aquariums. In addition, the cage and tubes can quickly become smelly if they are not cleaned frequently enough. Some portly Syrian hamsters can get stuck in the tubes, and some hamsters can readily gnaw through the plastic tubes and escape. The plastic can also become dirty and difficult to see through, so it must be regularly washed.

In response to these drawbacks, many manufacturers have redesigned these cages to provide much better ventilation and ease in cleaning. If you want a combination cage for your hamster, be sure to select a model with maximum ventilation. Before buying, check that the door is large enough for you to reach in and easily take out your pet.

Unsuitable Cages

Hamsters of all species are experts at escaping their enclosures. This means that the cage you choose must be well constructed and escape proof. A wooden cage is not recommended. Besides being able to chew their way out, wooden cages are difficult to keep clean, because wood absorbs urine and other odors.

Although they might look spacious and fun, the large two- and three-story cages sold for rats are not recommended for hamsters because their feet sometimes get caught in the wire platforms.

How to Help Your Hamster Adjust to His New Home

To help your hamster adjust to his new home, ask the pet store employee to place a small handful of shavings from the hamster's original cage into the container you are using to take your pet home. Place the old shavings into your pet's new home. The smell of his original home can help your hamster settle more comfortably into his new environment.

The rectangular plastic enclosures with snap-on lids, sometimes called small-animal habitats, are not typically large enough to house a single Syrian hamster or a pair of dwarf hamsters. They make suitable carrying cages to take your new pets home or to the veterinarian, and they provide a secure place to keep your pets while you are cleaning their cage, but they should not be a permanent home for dwarf hamsters. Be careful with these cages, because if you drop them, they will break.

Cage Placement

Your hamster should be part of your family. Place his cage in a location where you can watch and enjoy him. Make the cage a pleasant part of the room by placing it on a dresser or table with some attractive fabric beneath it. The floor is not the most ideal location, because the temperature near the floor is often cooler than on a dresser or table. On top of a high shelf is also not ideal, since it will be too high for you to enjoy your pet.

Do not place your pet's cage near a heating or air conditioning vent, a drafty window, or in direct sunlight. Dwarf hamsters are susceptible to overheating, chills, and drafts. Hamsters can tolerate a house's normal variations in room light, temperature, and humidity. Room temperatures between 65° and 72°F (18.3° and 22.2°C) with humidity between 40 and 50 percent represent satisfactory conditions.

Dwarf hamsters who live in cold homes can become torpid and

begin to hibernate. It is not recommended that you allow your hamster to become torpid. Such cool temperatures are unlikely to occur in a home, but they could exist in a garage—so never keep your pet in the garage. Not only is it unhealthy due to automobile exhaust, but the temperature is more extreme and variable, both too cold and too hot. Most importantly, your hamster is likely to be neglected.

Hamsters do not like bright lights. Therefore, do not place your pet's cage next to a table, floor, or overhead light. The enclosure should be placed out of the direct view of the family cat and dog, because your hamster can become nervous and stressed if a dog or cat consistently sniffs at and stares at him.

43

In addition, dwarf hamsters might be sensitive to the ultrasonic sounds produced by computers and televisions, so it's important that you not place his home near computers or televisions. Finally, hamsters are enthusiastic gnawers, so never leave any items such as clothing or papers on or near your pet's cage, since anything that can be pulled into the enclosure will be chewed and destroyed.

Cleaning the Cage

A clean cage plays an important role in keeping your hamster healthy. Plan on cleaning your pet's cage once or twice a week. The more hamsters kept in a cage, especially in a cage that is relatively small, the more often the cage will need to be cleaned. If your hamsters are housed in a very large cage,

This size cage would make a suitable carrying cage, not a permanent home.

The Stuff of Everyday Life

Hamsters of all species are experts at escaping their enclosures.

How to Clean the Cage

To clean your hamster's cage, completely change the bedding and replace it with fresh, clean bedding. You can do a partial cage change between cleanings.

Your hamster will establish one or two toilet areas in his enclosure, which can make cage cleaning easier. Try placing his food dish, water bottle, and nest box at one end of his cage. This will help him establish a bathroom area away from his sleeping and eating areas. If your pet does use a cage corner for a bathroom area, the bedding in this area can be replaced every few days or so. Doing so will help reduce odor and keep the cage cleaner and more sanitary.

You will need to place your pet in a secure container, such as a plastic carrying cage, while you clean his home. Some hamster owners place their pets within their nest box in the bathtub during cage cleaning. The nest box provides a secure hiding place, and the slippery sides of the bathtub are usually too steep for hamsters to jump or climb out.

Each week, partially or completely (if it smells or is dirty) replace the nesting material in each hamster's nest box. You will also need to wash or replace some of your pet's toys and his nest box when they become chewed and tattered. Sometimes these objects absorb urine odors and become smelly. Replacing them, rather than washing them, will greatly decrease any pungent smell.

Hamsters often become upset and frantically run around their home after it

such as a 20-gallon (75.7 L) aquarium, then it is reasonable to consider cleaning it every 7 to 10 days.

A hamster's small, hard droppings do not smell bad, but their urine can develop a pungent aroma due to the ammonia it produces. No hamster should be housed on dirty, wet bedding. Your hamster's cage will only smell if you do not clean it often enough. Ideally, you should clean your pet's cage before it becomes smelly. If the area around the enclosure smells offensive, it is past time to clean the cage.

Kids and Hamster Care

Owning a pet is one of the pleasures of childhood. Besides being fun, it is even beneficial. A pet can help teach children respect for other living creatures, showing them that a pet is not a toy and that he has needs separate from their own desires. For example, children should not handle the pet too much, and the pet must be allowed to sleep, even when they would rather take him out to play. Pets also allow children to assume responsibility and learn nurturing skills. They help children learn how to be compassionate, how to play gently, and what hurting means.

Unfortunately, these benefits are unlikely to occur without a parent's involvement. A child's age and maturity are important factors when deciding how much responsibility a child can assume. Parents of younger children must know that the hamster's welfare will be their responsibility, too. In fact, to a varying extent, a parent must participate in the care of a child's hamster. Such assistance might include driving to the pet store to buy fresh food, supervising playtime to ensure the safety of the child and hamster, or helping to clean a large cage that a small child has trouble managing. While it is understandable that busy parents do not welcome additional responsibilities, a hamster by himself will not teach a child to be responsible.

Because children cannot be expected to care for their hamster without supervision, it helps if a parent is enthusiastic about the pet. Simply by showing an interest, parents can encourage their child to care for their pet.

One veterinary reference manual, which describes common illnesses affecting small animals, lists a possible cause of sudden death in hamsters as starvation and/or dehydration. It is reasonable to assume that cases of neglect are probably primarily related to children being the primary caretaker for a hamster. It is imperative that parents participate in the care of their child's hamster and, depending on the child's age, supervise to ensure the pet's health and safety.

Ideally, you should clean your pet's cage before it becomes smelly.

has been cleaned. Although pet owners find the clean cage refreshing, hamsters are not often as enthusiastic. They like something with their scent on it and will often become quite busy marking their home so that it smells better to them. Partial cage cleanings, such as replacing most, but not all, of your hamster's bedding and nesting material and not washing all of his toys will satisfy his need for something familiar.

Once a month, do a thorough cleaning. Wash the cage with hot, soapy water. Be sure to rinse and dry it thoroughly. If necessary, disinfect the cage with a bleach solution. Immersing a cage for at least 30 seconds in a bleach solution, consisting of one

tablespoon (14.8 mL) of bleach for each gallon (L) of cold water, will kill any germs. Allow the cage to air dry afterward. Wash the water bottle, food dish, and any plastic toys as well. Wood toys can eventually splinter if washed in water, so scraping them clean with a file is effective. Finally, scrape or file off any grime that might have accumulated on the bars of a wire cage.

Making Cage Cleaning Easier

Instead of feeling overwhelmed with the weekly task of cleaning and thus postponing it, try using a kitty litter scoop to quickly remove and replace some of the soiled bedding. Doing so can allow the cage to remain sanitary a few extra days before you undertake a more meticulous cleaning. Other steps to make cage cleaning easier include buying larger quantities of bedding so that you always have some around for a quick change.

Nest Box

Each dwarf hamster needs a nesting box for sleeping and security. Keep in mind that many pet stores do not provide nest boxes for their small pets, to make the animals easier for you to see. Because the animals are only in the store for a brief time, no harm is done. However, in your home, this "bedroom" gives your pet a safe hiding place to retreat away from loud noises and any disturbing activity outside his cage.

Partial cage cleanings will satisfy your hamster's need for something familiar.

You can buy a nesting box at a pet store. A variety of types are available, including ones that are made to satisfy a small animal's natural instinct to chew, such as fruit-flavored cardboard tunnels, huts made from natural plant fibers, and wooden blocks that your pet can hollow out. Other kinds are less destructible and are made of ceramic or hard plastic. You can also make your pet a nest box from an old cereal box or cardboard milk carton. Once the box becomes chewed up or smelly, you must replace it.

Give your hamster unscented tissue paper or paper towels to shred into nesting material. Shredding paper into a nest is a favorite activity for these animals. Pet stores also sell nesting material that you can use. However, do not buy artificial fiber

Nest boxes can be made of ceramic or something simple like a cardboard box.

bedding sold for birds and hamsters. The small fibers can wrap around a hamster's feet, causing loss of the limb. Hamsters also stuff the material into their cheek pouches and sometimes have difficulty removing it. They can even eat the material and are unable to pass it out of their system.

Run-About Ball

Plastic run-about balls designed just for hamsters are a safe option for allowing your pet to exercise outside his cage. The minimum size to use for a Syrian hamster is 7 inches (17.8 cm). Dwarf hamsters need a smaller, lighter ball 5 to 6 inches (12.7 to 15.2 cm) in diameter. Only one hamster can be placed in a run-about ball at a time.

Always supervise your hamster when using this device, because falling down stairs, getting stuck in place, and other pets are potential hazards. Your hamster might also chew anything he can reach through the ventilation holes in the ball. If he stops on an electrical cord, for example, he can chew it and possibly electrocute himself. Some balls are designed to move on a race track, which helps to confine a hamster's movements to a safe place. These balls can also be used outside on a smooth lawn, but hamsters do not like bright light, and much of their activity in the ball is due to fear. Thus, you should only use a run-about ball inside your home.

If you have more than one Syrian hamster, it is best to provide each hamster with his own run-about ball. Some hamsters will become agitated and urinate and mark excessively when placed inside a ball that has been used by another individual. Even if you wash the ball, a hamster's keen sense of smell and territorial nature will cause him to be stressed.

Compared to a cage, run-about balls have little ventilation, so do not keep your pet confined in one for more than a half-hour at a time. When

tired, a hamster usually stops moving and sits in the ball. When he is finished, wash and dry the ball, and remember to do so after each use.

Toys

Toys give your hamster something to do and make him a more enjoyable pet. In general, hamsters housed with toys are more active and interesting to watch, and they are happier and more content. Without toys, your pet will become bored and listless.

Hamsters enjoy playing with almost anything you put in their cage. Their play involves scampering over the toys,

Always supervise your hamster when using the run-about ball.

darting in and out of tunnels, scent marking, and chewing the toys. Expect your pet's toys to be chewed and destroyed over time, so make sure that you offer safe items.

Pet stores sell a variety of toys that can be made into a playground for hamsters. Give your pet toys designed for hamsters and other small rodents, such as wood chew sticks, tunnels, and ladders. If your pet is housed in an aquarium, you can increase the area available for your hamster by adding ladders and platforms. Many wooden toys made for parakeets and parrots are safe to use. Wood chews keep hamsters busy and active and provide a hard surface for them to gnaw, which helps to keep their teeth in good shape. Tree branches from alder, willow, maple, ash, and apple trees are also safe for your hamster to chew—just make sure that the trees were not treated with any kind of chemical. Wood toys absorb urine and other odors and must be replaced when they become smelly and old.

Alternating toys is a trick that dog and cat owners have used for years and can be used by hamster owners as well. Let your hamsters play with a toy for a week, and then take it away and replace it with a new toy. The following week you can temporarily take away the new toy and replace it with the old one. By switching your pet's toys around, your hamster stays active and remains interested in exploring his environment.

Do not overcrowd your hamster's cage with toys. Not only does this leave little room for him, but he might become injured if a toy falls on him.

Water Bottle

Provide your hamster with fresh water using a gravity-fed water bottle sold at pet stores. A water bottle designed for hamsters is the best size to use for your pet. Choose a bottle with hatch marks

A ladder is a fun toy your hamster will love.

Provide your hamster with fresh water using a gravity-fed water bottle.

with his cage bedding. The water will become unsanitary and unsuitable for drinking. The increased moisture from a spilled dish of water can create an unhealthy, damp environment, especially in an aquarium-type cage.

(or make your own with an indelible marker) to help you monitor the amount of water your hamster drinks. He must always have water available. Ideally, you should empty and refill the water bottle every day, although most pet owners fill the bottle every other day.

The bottle's water tube should be a comfortable height for your hamster to easily reach up and drink from, but it should not be so low to the cage floor that bedding can touch the tube and cause the bottle to leak. To prevent leaks, the tip of the water bottle should not touch the cage bedding or any cage furniture. A special holder, also available at pet stores, enables you to hang the water bottle in an aquarium. In case the bottle leaks, do not place it over your pet's food dish or near his nest box.

Do not use an open dish to provide your hamster with water, because he will fill an open container of water

Homemade Toys

You can find suitable toys for your pet in your home. Give your hamster the cardboard roll from an empty toilet paper or paper towel roll. You can partially bury these tubes under your pet's bedding and create a system of tunnels for him to explore. Be creative and connect multiple rolls to make multiple entrances and exits. Cardboard (not Styrofoam) egg cartons also provide entertaining play for hamsters. Remember, they will chew on whatever you put in their cage, so be sure the items are safe.

Chapter 3

Good Eating

Like people, hamsters are omnivorous, which means that they eat both plant and animal foods. In the wild, hamsters will eat seasonally available seeds, including wheat, barley, millet, soybeans, and peas, as well as plant shoots, leaves, flowers, and root vegetables, including potatoes, carrots, and beets. Insects and other invertebrates such as spiders are also eaten and stored in a hamster's food chambers.

his chapter will help you to get a better understanding of nutrition and how to best feed your hamster for optimal health and longevity.

Basic Nutrition

Good nutrition is a key factor in promoting a long and healthy life for your hamster. A balanced diet for hamsters includes the appropriate amounts of carbohydrates, fats, minerals, proteins, vitamins, and water. All these nutrients interact in the building, maintenance, and functioning of a hamster's body.

Carbohydrates

Carbohydrates perform numerous functions, such as providing energy. Concentrated sources of carbohydrates include grains such as oats and corn.

Fats

Fat is a concentrated source of energy that provides twice as many calories per serving as protein or carbohydrates. A good diet for hamsters should contain approximately 5 percent fat. Fats make up part of the structure

Good nutrition is a key factor in promoting a long and healthy life.

of every cell and are necessary for the absorption of fat-soluble vitamins, including vitamins A, D, and E. Fats also help to prevent and alleviate skin problems. A deficiency of fat can show up as scaly skin or rough, thin hair.

Minerals

Minerals, which include calcium, phosphorous, sodium, and other chemical elements, are important in many body functions, such as the development of bones and teeth, muscle and nerve function, and proper water balance. A deficiency or excess can lead to serious medical problems. Trace elements, which include cobalt, copper, iodine, iron, manganese, selenium, and zinc, are necessary nutrients but only in very small amounts. Trace elements perform many functions, such as the role of iron in bringing oxygen to the body.

Proteins

Protein is needed for functions such as the growth and maintenance of muscle and the production of antibodies, hormones, and enzymes. The amount of protein that your pet needs is influenced by a number of physiological factors,

Coprophagy

Small animals such as rabbits and hamsters are hindgut fermenters. They digest much of their food in the cecum, which is located at the juncture of the small intestine and large intestine. This is the same location as a human's appendix. Beneficial bacteria and protozoa, called *microflora*, live in the hamster's digestive tract and help him digest food. These microorganisms produce various products or by-products of metabolism, including water-soluble vitamins and amino acids. The nutrients produced contribute substantially to a hamster's balanced diet. Some of the nutrients are directly absorbed into the hamster's gastrointestinal tract. However, many are not available to the animal unless he consumes special droppings that contain the nutrients synthesized by the bacteria, a practice called *coprophagy*. Hamsters typically engage in this behavior at night or early in the morning, when you are not likely to observe them. Sometimes called *night feces*, the hamster eats the soft feces directly from the anus, so normally you will never see them. Nonetheless, do not be concerned if you see your pets engaged in such behavior. Leave them alone, because coprophagy is necessary for their good health. Although this seems unpleasant, digesting the food a second time allows the hamster to obtain the most nutrition from it. Cows also digest their food a second time, but they chew cud that comes up from their stomach.

such as age and reproductive status. Hamsters need less protein when they are adults than they do when they are growing or if they are pregnant or nursing a litter of babies. A good diet for hamsters should contain between 16 and 20 percent protein.

Vitamins

Vitamins are necessary as catalysts for chemical reactions in the body. They are important in preventing diseases and in regulating functions such as growth and blood clotting. Vitamins are classified as water soluble or as fat soluble. The vitamins that hamsters need to eat in their diet are different from those needed by people. For example,

hamsters can make their own vitamin C, while people must get it from an external source such as oranges.

Water

Water is essential for all the physiological functions in your pet's body. A pet hamster cannot survive without water, so yours should always have water available. The amount of water that hamsters drink each day depends on the moisture in their food. If you provide your hamsters with small amounts of fresh fruits, vegetables, and live insect foods, they will drink less water.

A dwarf hamster will typically drink less than 5 milliliters of water each day,

while Syrian hamsters will drink less than 20 milliliters a day. Many water bottles are sold with milliliter or ounce markings on them. (There are approximately 29.5 milliliters in 1 ounce.) Such markings are useful to track your hamster's water consumption. If the amount of water in the bottle does not seem to decrease over a day or so, check to see whether the metal spout is clogged with bedding.

Ideally, you should change your hamster's water every day. However, most pet owners do not find this practical or convenient. At the very least, completely change the water in your hamster's bottle once a week. It might be necessary to change the water more often if you have more than

two hamsters in a cage. Select a water bottle that is large enough so that your hamsters do not run out of water. The standard hamster bottle provides sufficient water to last two hamsters for most of the week.

It is important to give the water bottle a good cleaning at least once a week. Even if the bottle looks clean, it is probably slimy on the inside and contaminated with bacteria and other harmful pathogens. Use a slender bristle brush to clean the slimy residue that will coat the bottle. Check to see that the stopper is not clogged with bedding. Some hamsters nibble the metal water spout, so check to be sure that no jagged ends are present that could cut your pet. If there are, you will need to replace the water bottle.

A pet hamster cannot survive without water, so yours should always have water available.

Reading Labels

Hamster foods sold in pet stores are formulated to be nutritionally complete. The items that compose a food are stated in the ingredients list and are listed in descending order by weight. The first three to five items on an ingredient list make up most of the food. A nutritious food will be composed primarily of seeds and grains, with only a small amount of fatty nuts, such as sunflower seeds.

It is important that the food you feed your hamsters is fresh.

On every bag of hamster food is a guaranteed analysis that gives the percentage of nutrients such as protein, fat, fiber, and calcium, as well as moisture. The protein and fat contents are usually listed as minimums, while the amount of fiber and calcium are typically given as both minimums and maximums. The word *crude*, which precedes each measure, refers to laboratory analysis rather than digestibility. Even commercial treats sold at pet stores provide basic nutritional information on protein, fat, fiber, and moisture content.

Knowing the nutritional composition of a food can help you prevent and manage some health problems that afflict pet hamsters, such as obesity and diabetes. For example, an overweight hamster should be fed a food that is low in fat, while a diabetic hamster should be fed a high-fiber diet with no sugary treats, such as dried fruits.

Types of Food

It is important that the food you feed your hamsters is fresh. Food that is old can become stale and lose some of its nutritional value. Packaged foods should be fresh and sweet-smelling, not rancid or dusty. Do not buy a large amount of food, because it will take too long to use all of it.

Check to see whether an expiration date is printed on the package of food. Some manufacturers stamp a date on food bags and recommend that the food be used within 1 year of this date. Typically, the freshest, best-quality packaged food is found at busy pet and feed stores that constantly rotate their stock.

Proper storage of your hamster's food is essential. Store the food in a cool, dry environment. Exposure to sunlight, heat, and time degrade the vitamins in a food. Also, keep your pet's food in an airtight container, such as a glass jar with a lid, or be sure to completely close a package that is self-sealing. This will keep the food fresh and prevent it from spoiling.

The Expert Knows

Supplements

Feeding your hamster a fresh, high-quality diet consisting of a commercial food, some hay, and a variety of fresh vegetables and fruits will usually ensure adequate intake of necessary vitamins and minerals. Your hamster will also obtain vitamins from the ingestion of cecal pellets. Unless your veterinarian recommends a vitamin and mineral supplement for a specific condition, most hamsters do not require supplements.

eat. A hamster usually turns a mealworm or cricket in his hands so that he consumes the head first before eating the remainder of the insect. Not all hamsters will eat live foods, though; some become frightened and want nothing to do with the insect.

Because dwarf hamsters are small, you should offer them regular-sized mealworms, not the giant type. Feed live foods as a treat, only one or two every few days.

Packaged Food

Feeding your hamsters a healthy, balanced diet is considerably easier than it was 75 years ago, because a variety of commercial foods are sold for hamsters at pet stores.

Feed your hamsters one of the

The following is a description of the different types of food that your hamster may enjoy.

Live Foods

Hamsters like eating live moths, mealworms, and crickets. You can catch live moths for your pets from a porch light turned on at night in the summer. Many hamsters will eagerly expend quite a bit of energy chasing and catching the live moths you put in their cage.

Both crickets and mealworms are sold at pet stores for reptiles. It is fascinating to watch a hamster pounce on a mealworm or chase after and catch a cricket to

A variety of commercial foods are available for your hamster.

rodent mixes sold at pet stores for hamsters and gerbils. These mixes contain seeds, grains, beans, nuts, alfalfa pellets, dried fruits and vegetables, and sometimes various types of kibble. Do not choose a food that is mostly sunflower seeds or other nuts, because such a diet will cause your hamsters to become malnourished and overweight.

Hamsters enjoy picking through their food and eating their favorite items first. Since a food's nutritional analysis is based on consumption of the entire mix of ingredients, a selective eater may not be getting a nutritious, complete diet. Over time, this "selective feeding" can cause inadequate nutrition and obesity. While it is reasonable not to expect your hamsters to like some items in their food, consistently refusing to eat more than half of a food's ingredients is not healthy. You can thwart your hamsters' selective feeding by not offering them more food until they have to eat the less tasty items remaining in their food dish or pantry.

Some hamster breeders also offer their pets nutritionally complete laboratory blocks or pellets made specifically for hamsters and other rodents. These types of food contain a balance of all the nutrients a hamster needs. In addition, they are convenient and easy to feed. The ingredients in these blocks are blended so that a hamster cannot pick out one ingredient, and he will therefore consume adequate nutrients. The blocks are usually low in fat, typically

less than 5 percent, compared with 40 percent fat in sunflower seeds. Lab blocks do not always fit in a hamster's cheek pouches and must be carried to their pantry with their teeth. In addition to the lab blocks, then, your pet still needs a hamster mix so that he can engage in his natural behavior of carrying food in his cheek pouches to the pantry.

Hay

Hamsters need fiber, and many enjoy eating loose hay rather than eating the alfalfa pellets found in most hamster mixes. Besides essential fiber, hay gives your pet something to do. You can place the hay on the floor of your pet's cage or keep it in a hay rack that attaches to the side of a wire cage. You can also stuff some hay into a toilet-paper tube. Making your hamster work for his food helps to keep him active and healthy.

Your hamster will greet with delight any treats that you give him—and tasty treats are a great way to win his confidence. It can be fun shopping for hamster treats in a pet store, because such a great variety is available. Commercial hamster treats include honey-coated seed and nut sticks, dehydrated fruit and vegetable puffs, and nut cakes.

Some treats come in attractive shapes and colors designed to appeal to people, not hamsters. Their packages often claim that the product is healthful and nutritious. However, many of these treats, such as yogurt drops, are just like junk food for people and are high in fat, carbohydrates, and sugar. They should only be offered on special occasions.

Some treats sold at pet stores are designed to help create a more interesting environment for your hamster. Seed treat sticks, hay cubes, and millet sprays (in the bird section of pet stores) hung in the cage keep hamsters busy. To prevent overindulgence, hang the treats in the cage for 5 or 10 minutes, and then remove them. Offer them again the following evening.

Other treats to try offering your hamster include dry, unsweetened cereals such as toasted whole grain oat cereal, crispy rice cereal, and shredded wheat cereal. Your pet will also enjoy pretzels, crackers, stale bread, hard, uncooked noodles, uncooked rice, and uncooked hot cereals (for example, cracked four-grain cereal). Many hamsters love dog biscuits, but be cautious about offering any of your dog's regular kibble, because some brands are high in fat. These treats and the hard foods in your hamster's regular diet, will help to keep his teeth trim.

If your pet is housed in a wire cage, do not feed him treats through the cage bars. Otherwise, anything (including a finger) that is poked through the cage bars might get nipped. Always open the cage door to offer a treat. In addition, wash your hands before handling your hamster, because any food smells on your hands can cause your pet to nip.

Remember, moderation is the key when feeding your hamster treats. Your pet should not eat so many treats that he has no appetite for his regular food.

Most large pet stores sell a variety of hay in small, convenient packages. There are two types of hay: grass and legume. Grass hay includes orchard grass, oat hay, timothy, and mixed grass. Legume hay includes alfalfa and clover. Hamsters usually prefer the tastier leaves and stems of alfalfa hay compared to grass hay. If loose hay is unavailable, cubed hay is another option worth trying.

Apples are just one of the many fruits your hamster can enjoy.

Vegetables and Fruits

In addition to your hamster's regular diet of grains, seeds, and laboratory blocks, you can offer him small amounts of fresh fruits and vegetables. Hamsters relish fruits and vegetables, and these foods provide important variety and nutrients in your pet's diet. You can also use a small piece of tasty vegetable or fruit to bond with your pet during playtime and training.

Before offering these fruits and vegetables, be sure to wash and dry them. Offer your hamster no more than .5 teaspoon (2.5 mL) of fresh foods. By using this conservative estimate, your pet is less likely to experience any

problems, such as diarrhea. Also, this amount will ensure that your hamster is able to comfortably hold the treat in his paws; the portion size should never be so large that he cannot fit it into his cheek pouches. Keep in mind that many photographs in pet books showing hamsters with whole strawberries or carrots were staged. After the photograph was taken, the food treat was likely removed before the hamster could overeat.

Ideally, your hamster should immediately eat the fresh food item that you offer him. However, many dwarf hamsters prefer to stuff the

Carrots are safe for your hamster to nibble on.

items into their cheek pouches and add them to their pantry. If your hamster does not eat his fresh food right away, it could spoil. Each evening, before you offer your pet more fresh food, check his pantry and nest and remove any uneaten fresh items. Moist food left in the cage can become putrid, and bacteria and mold can grow on it, which could make your hamster sick. Hard vegetables and fruits such as carrots and apples are enjoyed by hamsters and are less likely to spoil than are soft, moist items such as cucumbers and berries.

Offer previously untried foods in very small pieces to make sure that your hamster likes it and to make sure it will not cause digestive upset. Feeding a large amount can lead to digestive upset and cause acute diarrhea in your hamster. Feed only one type of vegetable or fruit at a time, and wait several days before offering

another kind. This way, you will know if a particular type of food causes problems. Symptoms of indigestion include bloating and lethargy. If a vegetable or fruit causes indigestion or diarrhea, do not feed it to your hamster.

Hamsters who regularly consume fresh foods in their daily diet are less likely to experience digestive upset than hamsters who are rarely fed such foods. If you have not offered fruits or vegetables in a while, always err on the safe side by offering very tiny pieces.

Safe Fruits and Vegetables

Hamsters enjoy a variety of vegetables, including carrots, broccoli, peas, spinach, squash, peppers, corn, and green beans. They can safely eat just about any kind of fruit, including kiwis, peaches, tomatoes, watermelon, apple, peach, plum, pear, melon, raspberry, papaya, blueberry, blackberry, strawberry, and pineapple. Relatively inexpensive fruits such as bananas, grapes, and oranges are other options. Small amounts of dried fruits such as

banana chips and raisins can also be offered. Remove the seeds of apples, which are poisonous, before feeding your pet. You should also remove any large fruit seed pits before feeding your pet the fruit. Although the pits can help your hamster keep his teeth trim, the "nut" inside the hard shell can sometimes be poisonous, as is the case with apricot pits. Some hamsters also like green wheat shoots (sold as cat greens at pet stores).

Unhealthy Foods

Although it can be fun to offer your hamster new types of food and see if he enjoys them, not all foods are good for hamsters. Do not feed your pet junk food made for people. Although hamsters will greedily eat potato chips and eagerly look for more, potato chips, cookies, candy, and other snack foods are not healthy for your pet. Sweet, sticky foods, including moist dried fruits, can become stuck in a hamster's cheek pouches and should not be offered. Also, avoid feeding high-fat foods, such as the seed and nut mixes sold for parrots and cockatiels.

It is best to feed your hamster the same amount of food at the same time each day.

Vegetables That You Shouldn't Feed

There are some vegetables that you should not feed your pet because they can cause gastrointestinal upset. Even if your hamster seems to eat these vegetables without noticeable problems, it is still best not to include them. Fresh foods to avoid feeding your pet include raw iceberg lettuce, kidney beans, onions, peanut butter, raw potatoes, and rhubarb. Although they are not something you would normally feed your pet, be aware that many houseplants are poisonous to hamsters. Never give your pet any part of a houseplant to snack on.

How Much to Feed

Your hamster should always have dry food in his dish or pantry. Even though he is primarily nocturnal, your pet will still nibble on food during the day. If his dish or pantry is empty, increase the amount of food you feed. Conversely, if your hamster's food pantry becomes too large, you are feeding too much. The amount your pet eats will vary depending on what type of food you feed. Typically, hamsters eat less of the laboratory blocks than they do of the rodent mixes.

Most hamsters stop eating when they have consumed enough calories. Any marked loss or increase in a

Children and Feeding

Parents should not give their child tasks that are too difficult. Preschool-age children (3 to 5 years) can help with simple tasks such as pouring pre-measured food into the hamster's dish. Elementary-age children (6 to 9 years) can assume more responsibility. For example, they can feed and water the hamster and remind their parents when fresh supplies are needed. Children 10 and older can usually assume almost full responsibility for their hamster, although their parents should still oversee the pets' care to make sure that he is not neglected.

hamster's appetite could signal illness. Every few days, check on your pet's pantry to ensure that the food is not damp or moldy, and be sure to discard stored food at each weekly cleaning.

How much your hamster needs to eat will change throughout his life. In fact, the amount will vary according to his age, gender, and activity level. Young, growing hamsters will need to eat more food per gram of body weight than do adults. Also, because male hamsters are larger than females, they need to eat more food than do females.

Hamsters who run around and play on regularly rotated toys will require more food than animals who just sit in their cage with few toys and little to do. Pregnant or nursing hamsters obviously eat more food.

When to Feed

It is best to feed your hamster the same amount of food at the same time each day. Because these animals are nocturnal and most active at night, you should feed your hamster in the evening rather than in the morning. Also, try to feed your hamster at the same time each day, such as when you come home from school or work or after your own dinnertime.

The obvious satisfaction and delight that hamsters take when sorting through a fresh dish of food makes feeding a rewarding time to observe your pet. Watching him eat, even for a few minutes, will help you determine that he is active and well.

65

Good Eating

Looking Good

If you are looking for a pet who requires little in the way of grooming, a hamster is a good choice. These little rodents are naturally clean and need very little, if any, assistance from their owner to stay that way.

Brushing

Hamsters do not need to be brushed. Sometimes the hair around a Syrian hamster's hip glands might appear wet or greasy, but this is nothing to be concerned about. Your pet will use the scent to mark his cage and cage furniture.

All furry animals shed hair, including hamsters. However, unlike some other small animal pets, such as rabbits, hamsters do not undergo a noticeable molt. A hamster's hair is so short and fine that you are unlikely to ever notice any shed hair in or near his cage.

Bedding sometimes clings to the fluffy coat of long-haired Syrian hamsters. Although it might look untidy, the bedding does not usually cause the hair to become tangled and matted. If you wish, you can gently brush a long-haired hamster using a small, soft kitten brush or a toothbrush. However, once your pet returns to his home, the bedding usually sticks to his hair again.

Although it is unnecessary, brushing can be an enjoyable way to bond with your hamster, whether he has long or short hair. Some hamsters like this attention, while others do not. If your hamster holds still while you gently brush him, assume he likes it. On the other hand, if he always struggles and runs away, it should be obvious that he does not like being brushed.

A clean cage is one of the most important ways that you can help your hamster stay clean and well-groomed. If a hamster is dirty and smells, it is usually because he has been living on dirty bedding. Clean the cage, provide fresh, sweet-

Although it is not necessary, brushing can be an enjoyable way to bond with your hamster.

Washing your hamster can cause him to get sick.

Looking Good

smelling bedding, and allow your hamster to groom himself.

Bathing

Your hamster will never need a bath with water and shampoo. Washing your hamster can cause him to get sick, even if you use warm water and dry him with a towel. Using a hair dryer is even worse, because you can accidentally burn your pet, not to mention increase his stress level astronomically.

If your pet has gotten into something sticky, he can usually clean his coat by himself. If necessary, you can help his grooming by carefully trimming away any sticky hair. To prevent accidentally cutting his skin, do not use scissors larger than the small type made for cutting people's nails. You can also spot-clean his sticky fur with the corner of a warm, damp washcloth. Immediately use a paper towel or a dry cloth to absorb the moisture.

easily reach themselves. A hamster who cannot keep himself clean is probably sick and should be examined by a veterinarian.

Nail Care

Just like your nails, the nails of your hamster grow continuously. Trimming your pet's nails is not necessary to keep your hamster healthy and happy, unlike other small pets such as rabbits and guinea pigs, whose nails must be routinely trimmed. Most hamsters chew and clip their own nails to keep them short. While his nails can be sharp, you should rarely notice them if you properly handle your pet.

Sometimes, a hamster's nails can get caught in the wire floor of a cage or on a carpet. During his struggles, he might rip the nail or tear it out by the root. The damaged nail bed often turns black but usually heals on its own. Sometimes the nail will regrow, although in other cases, the nail will never regrow. This is not a cause for concern unless you notice redness or swelling of the toe, which could indicate an infection.

If you think that your hamster needs his nails cut, it is best to have a veterinarian perform the procedure and show you how to do so. Cutting a hamster's nails can often be difficult, and if done improperly, painful and traumatic. Because hamsters are so small and wiggly, it is very easy to slip and accidentally cut the toe. Hamsters must be restrained during nail cutting, and you don't want your

Hair Trimming

It is not usually necessary to cut a Syrian hamster's long hair. However, exceptions do occur. Some pet owners have found their hamster's long hair gets caught in the exercise wheel's spindle, and some senior long-haired hamsters no longer groom themselves as diligently.

If you must trim your pet's coat, keep in mind that hamsters, like people, have very thin skin. It is very easy to cut a hamster's skin as well as his fur. Besides being extremely painful and possibly requiring a trip to the veterinarian, your hamster will become frightened of you, and it will take a long time to win back his trust.

Hamsters spend up to 20 percent of their waking hours grooming themselves. They wash their face with their front paws, delicately clean each ear with their hind toes, nibble clean their toes, and wash their front and backside with their tongues. Social dwarf hamsters will also groom each other, especially in places they cannot

pet to associate you with this unpleasant experience.

Cutting a hamster's nails can often be difficult.

Nonetheless, if you believe that it is necessary to cut your pet's nails, use clippers designed for birds or cats. Make sure the clippers are sharp, because they will make the task much easier. Keep cotton swabs and some type of styptic powder nearby to stop any bleeding. The best time to trim your hamster's nails is when he is sluggish and sleepy, not when he is wide awake. Two people are necessary for this task; one person should hold the hamster, and the other should clip the nails. The individual who holds the hamster should be the person with whom the hamster is most familiar. This person should pet the hamster, talk softly to him, and keep her hands away from his mouth in case he is accidentally hurt and bites.

Before attempting to cut your hamster's nails, be certain that you know where the quick ends, which is the living portion of the nail that contains nerves and blood vessels. The quick can sometimes be hard to detect in hamsters with dark-colored nails, but if you look underneath the nail, you can usually see where it ends. The nail should be cut

The Expert Knows

Dust Baths

Wild hamsters take dust baths to help keep themselves clean and to control external parasites. Some pet hamsters will also take dust baths. You can use chinchilla dust (usually volcanic ash) or bird gravel for this purpose. Use a container deep enough to hold about .5 inch (1.3 cm) of dust and large enough so that the hamsters can somersault and flip around in the dust. A glass or hard plastic container with sides about 2 inches (5.1 cm) high works well. Place the dust bowl in the cage for a short time once a week, and replace the dust after two or three baths. It is very entertaining to watch hamsters take a dust bath!

Your hamster's eyes do not need any routine care.

below the quick so that you don't cut into it and injure your pet. If the nail is trimmed too short, nicking the quick, it can cause painful bleeding, and your hamster will bite. One small cut is adequate—just enough to remove the sharp, pointed tip of the nail. If you accidentally nick the quick, blot it with a cotton swab and treat the bleeding with styptic powder.

Ear Care

A hamster can keep his ears clean without any help from you. The only time you need to examine your pet's ears is if you notice him scratching excessively at them or if they appear red and inflamed.

Hamsters sometimes get ear mites. If left untreated, mite infestations can cause serious problems. Take your hamster to a veterinarian if you notice excessive scratching or heavy wax buildup, discharge, redness, swelling, or odor from the ear. The vet will be able to dispense the most effective treatment and advice. Do not automatically assume that any discharge is from ear mites and treat with an over-the-counter ear mite

Kids and Grooming

One of the reasons that hamsters are popular pets for children is that they require very little in the way of grooming from their owners. One task that most children enjoy doing is offering their pets a dust bath. Otherwise, hamsters are able to keep themselves tidy.

medication. Accurate, professional diagnosis of the condition will speed your hamster's recovery and save him from discomfort and pain.

Eye Care

Your hamster's eyes do not need any routine care. Sometimes small particles from dusty bedding might irritate your pet's eyes. If you notice that your hamster is squinting his eye, or if the fur near his eyes is wet or discolored, something is wrong. You can moisten a cotton swab with lukewarm water and clean the area, but be very careful not to injure your wiggly hamster's eyes. If the condition does not improve by the next day, your hamster should see a veterinarian.

The eyes of older hamsters sometimes become cloudy due to cataracts, which will lead to blindness. No treatment is available, but most older hamsters are still able to navigate around their homes.

73

Hamsters don't require much grooming.

Chapter 5

Feeling Good

When purchased from a good source and provided with proper, loving care, hamsters are hardy little animals who don't get sick often. In fact, most pet hamsters live healthy lives without ever requiring a visit to the veterinarian. These animals do not need an annual "wellness exam," and they do not require vaccinations.

Finding a Veterinarian

For a hamster to receive the proper treatment, he needs the correct diagnosis. A veterinarian who routinely treats rodents and has a special interest in their care is best qualified and will most likely have the necessary hamster-sized equipment. Such individuals are more likely to be aware of advances and changes in treatment protocol.

To locate a veterinarian who is knowledgeable about rodents, call different veterinarians' offices and ask if they will treat hamsters. You can also inquire at pet stores, critter clubs, and humane societies.

Even if you don't expect your hamster to ever need a veterinarian's care, accidents happen that can require immediate medical attention for your pet. It is prudent to take a few minutes to find a veterinarian who treats rodents before you need one. Not all veterinarians treat these small pets, and you do not want to waste time in an emergency calling around to find a hamster doctor.

Cost

Even when you recognize that your hamster is "under the weather," you might hesitate to take your pet to a veterinarian due to the potential expense. A visit to a veterinarian can be costly, and you might find it difficult to spend large sums of money on a hamster who only cost a small sum. Some hamster owners will spend whatever it takes to treat their well-loved pets, but others are reluctant to do so. Discuss potential costs with your veterinarian beforehand, so that you will have a better idea how much your hamster's care might cost. Although it might be hard to put a price on your pet, in some cases, it might be necessary to decide how much you can afford to spend.

Be cautious about seeking diagnosis advice from friends, pet store employees, or the Internet before taking your hamster to a veterinarian. Although they might be

Signs of Emergency

The following symptoms indicate that a hamster needs immediate emergency care. Don't wait to see what happens, or it could be too late.

- Bleeding
- Broken bone
- Constipation
- Loss of appetite, refusing to eat
- Noticeable salivation
- Paralysis
- Rapid or labored breathing
- Runny, crusty eyes
- Seizures
- Sitting hunched, reluctant to move
- Watery diarrhea

describe his housing and what you feed him. If his cage is small enough, you can use it to transport him to the veterinarian. This is often less stressful, because your hamster remains in his familiar home. If the cage is too large, use a plastic small-animal habitat sold at pet stores. Place some of your pet's bedding in the carrying cage, as well as a cardboard tube or nest box in which your hamster can hide. Partially covering his regular cage or carrying cage with a towel can help your pet to feel more secure.

Because dogs and cats will likely be in the veterinary clinic's waiting room, it is best to wait to bring your pet into the clinic until the veterinarian is ready to see you. After checking in, remaining with your pet in a temperature-controlled car can reduce the stress he will feel when he senses these potential predators.

General Signs of Illness

Knowing a hamster's normal behavior will help you recognize when your pet might be sick. In fact, experienced pet owners and breeders are adept at

helpful and able to give an educated guess on what is wrong with your pet, the expertise, diagnostic skills, and medication needed to treat your hamster are only available from a veterinarian.

The Vet Visit

If you do need to take your hamster to the veterinarian, be prepared to

Knowing a hamster's normal behavior will help you recognize when your pet might be sick.

recognizing when a pet is sick. As you gain experience caring for your hamster, you will also become more proficient.

Sick hamsters generally present a similar range of symptoms. Obvious signs of illness include discharge from the eyes or nose. Sudden changes in behavior such as lethargy, reduced appetite, and failure to groom can also indicate illness. Signs of disease that are more difficult to detect include rough hair, hunched posture, and weight loss. Particular attention should be paid if a hamster is sensitive when touched on certain part of his

body, as this could indicate an injury from being dropped or squeezed. Any of these symptoms suggest that something might be wrong with your hamster, and a visit to the veterinarian might be prudent.

Most hamsters who are sick need to be treated immediately by a veterinarian. This is especially important, because pet owners often do not notice symptoms in their pet until their animal is very ill. In fact, by the time a pet owner realizes that her animal is ill, the hamster has usually been sick for quite some time.

In many cases, treatment is difficult because the condition is so advanced at the time of detection. Although some diseases progress rapidly and an affected pet can die within 24 hours, early recognition of a sick hamster may mean the difference between life and death for your pet.

Hamster Ailments

The ailments that can affect hamsters can be classified into four categories: trauma-induced injuries, infectious diseases, noninfectious diseases, and improper husbandry. The reasons that a hamster becomes sick are often a combination of factors from more than one category. For example, a poorly ventilated cage can create a noxious-smelling environment with high levels of ammonia that can cause an outbreak of a latent respiratory disease. Numerous factors affect how sick the hamster will become. These factors include the virulence of the pathogen, the hamster's age, dietary deficiencies, and whether the hamster is already sick with another illness.

Trauma-Induced Injuries

A traumatic injury is caused when a hamster is dropped, sat on, squashed behind a door or a piece of furniture, falls

Stress

"Stress" is a catch-all word for a variety of conditions that disturb or interfere with a hamster's normal physiological equilibrium. Because stress often leads to illness, it is frequently mentioned as a detrimental, contributing factor to various diseases. Besides becoming sick, a hamster can exhibit signs of stress in other ways, such as nervousness, lack of appetite, hair loss, and loose droppings.

A hamster can experience stress from pain and fear, a change in diet, exposure to temperature fluctuations, and/or when moving to a new cage. The trip from a pet store or a breeder to a new home can also be frightening and stressful for hamsters. Once in their new home, some hamsters settle down right away, while others take longer to adjust. Other stressful situations include loud noises, overcrowding, and harassment by dogs, cats, ferrets, or other pets. Groups of hamsters housed together can fight and injure each other. Fighting and bullying is particularly stressful for the animal who is always picked on, because he is at the bottom of the pecking order. Another source of stress occurs from inadequate food and water due to a pet owner's neglect (usually a child).

In short, stress can be a major factor in the development of what might otherwise remain a dormant disease. Therefore, it is wise to minimize the stress in your hamster's life.

Sudden changes in behavior can indicate illness.

from a height, or is squeezed while being held. If a hamster is injured—especially if he appears to be in pain—you should bring him to a veterinarian right away. The vet can determine whether the injury can be treated or whether it is kinder to put the hamster out of his misery with euthanasia.

The following are some common trauma-induced injuries.

Abscesses

An abscess is usually due to a secondary bacterial infection from a bite wound inflicted during a fight, or it could be caused by the infection of a cut. Some experienced hamster breeders are able to treat abscesses by using pressure to drain them. However, this can be gruesome, and a veterinarian is the preferred route to tend to an abscess. Using a needle, the veterinarian will biopsy (or sample) the abscess, then drain and clean the site. Usually a topical antibiotic is applied to the area.

The bacteria that cause an abscess are often opportunistic and can infect other organs besides the skin, so it is important that an affected hamster be properly treated. A veterinarian might deem it necessary to *culture,* or grow, a sample of the fluid to identify the type of bacteria present. An antibiotic selected on the basis of these test results is likely to be highly effective.

Broken Bones

Proper handling is key to avoiding trauma to your hamster.

Broken bones are a potential hazard, because hamsters can accidentally jump from your hands if something frightens them. Properly holding and playing with your hamsters can prevent such injuries from occurring. Depending on which bone is broken, an experienced veterinarian can often splint a broken bone.

Fight Injuries

Injuries from fights among hamsters can sometimes occur. Because infection from bacteria is always possible when a hamster is bitten in a fight, clean any bloody injuries with warm water

and an antiseptic or hydrogen peroxide. Watch the wounds and, if you detect any prolonged swelling or an abscess at the site of the bite wound, take your hamster to the veterinarian.

Infectious Diseases

Infectious diseases can spread from one animal to another and are caused by bacteria, viruses, and protozoa. Sometimes, the diseases caused by these agents are subclinical, meaning that signs of infection are difficult to detect. Individual animals also differ in their resistance to infectious organisms. Some exposed animals never display any symptoms. However, stress or other bacterial or viral infections can cause an animal to suddenly show symptoms.

A single pet is less at risk for infectious diseases compared with a pet who is housed in close proximity

FAMILY-FRIENDLY TIP

Kids and Hamster Care

Parents can help their child take better care of a hamster by teaching them to take an active interest in the hamster's welfare. Occasionally watching while a child plays with the hamster is not only a bonding experience, but the parent can help remind the child to keep track of any changes in their pet's health.

to large numbers of other animals of the same species. Fortunately, infectious diseases are often preventable through good husbandry.

The following are some common infectious diseases.

Pneumonia and Colds
If you observe the symptoms of a respiratory infection, such as sneezing,

Zoonotic Diseases

Zoonotic diseases are diseases that can be transmitted from animals to people. Your veterinarian will be aware of zoonotic diseases such as Salmonella and ringworm and can help you take preventive measures if your hamster is diagnosed with such an illness. The potential for disease transmission is reduced with proper hygiene, such as washing your hands after playing with your hamster and cleaning his cage. Purchasing your hamster from a clean environment, rather than a smelly, dirty one also reduces the chance of him having a zoonotic disease.

Although it is possible for people to contract some ailments from hamsters, this occurrence is rare.

wheezing, difficulty breathing, eyelids glued shut, discharge from the nose, lack of appetite, weight loss, and lethargy, immediately bring your hamster to a veterinarian. Pneumonia caused by bacteria can be treated with antibiotics, but the cure rate is still low.

Tyzzer's Disease
This is a highly contagious disease that is caused by bacteria (*Clostridium piliforme*). The disease is usually fatal. Symptoms include a scruffy coat, lack of activity, diarrhea, and dehydration, although some hamsters have no obvious signs before death. Sudden death or death after a short period of illness are often indicative of this disease.

If one of your hamsters exhibits the symptoms of this disease, immediately separate the healthy hamsters from the sick hamster. Place the sick animal in a covered carrying cage, and take him to your veterinarian. Treatment with the appropriate antibiotics can sometimes save the sick pet. If your veterinarian suspects Tyzzer's disease, antibiotics will be provided for all of your pets.

At this time, accurate diagnosis of Tyzzer's disease can only be made by a veterinarian pathologist's examination of the dead hamster. Poor husbandry and stress are implicated in this disease. Prevention is easier than treatment, but fortunately, this disease is rare in well-cared-for hamsters.

Wet Tail
The technical name for wet tail is *proliferative ileitis*. Various bacteria

Feeling Good

have been implicated as the causative agent. Symptoms of wet tail are diarrhea, and young hamsters are most susceptible. This disease is best treated by a veterinarian, who will prescribe antibiotics, administer fluids, and possibly force-feed the hamster. Over-the-counter medications can be effective for some types of diarrhea, but not diarrhea due to wet tail. Because you cannot know the cause of your pet's diarrhea, prompt veterinary treatment is important, because this disease can be fatal even with veterinary care.

Noninfectious Diseases

Noninfectious diseases are not typically transmitted from one hamster to another. The following is a description of some of the noninfectious diseases that hamsters can contract.

Diabetes

Diabetes is a chronic disease caused by either insufficient production of insulin or by resistance of organs to the effects of insulin. This disease has been documented in Campbell's Russian hamsters. Symptoms include excessive thirst and copious urination. At this

time, treatment options for dwarf hamsters are limited to changes in diet. Your veterinarian can best advise you on a course of treatment.

Glaucoma

Glaucoma affects a hamster's eyes and can result in blindness. This disease has been documented in Winter White hamsters. No cure exists for this affliction, although a veterinarian can sometimes prescribe eye drops to relieve the pain caused

Glaucoma has been documented in Winter White hamsters.

by the condition. Responsible breeders do not use affected hamsters for breeding.

Impacted Cheek Pouches

Sometimes an item, such as fluffy bedding or unsuitable sticky food, becomes stuck to the cheek pouch's lining. A veterinarian can remove the item with forceps or by flushing the cheek pouch. If a hamster seems unable to empty his cheek pouches, as evidenced by lumpy pouches, veterinary treatment is also necessary. Sharp items can pierce the hamster's cheek pouch, which can lead to infection, abscess, or an everted cheek pouch (turned inside out). Any of these conditions should be treated by a veterinarian.

Lumps and Bumps

A lump under your hamster's skin could be a tumor or an abscess. Your pet must be seen by a veterinarian, who can determine if the lump is a tumor and whether it is cancerous. Surgery might be necessary to remove the growth.

Teeth Problems

Although not common, the teeth of some hamsters need veterinary attention due to malocclusion. Malocclusion occurs when a hamster's incisor teeth do not meet properly, either because the teeth are overgrown or because they are misaligned.

A hamster's teeth can fail to meet and wear properly for several reasons.

Antibiotics

Infectious diseases that are caused by bacteria are treated with antibiotics. However, hamsters are sensitive to the effects of antibiotics. Some of these drugs can be harmful because they completely destroy or alter the useful bacteria that normally live in a hamster's digestive system (sometimes referred to as good bacteria or gut flora). Both conditions can lead to death. Luckily, you don't need to worry about which antibiotics are safe for your hamster, because your veterinarian will know what types of antibiotics can be safely used, as well as the recommended dosages and for what conditions. You should carefully monitor your hamster while he is being treated with an antibiotic and immediately report any decline in health to your veterinarian.

85

Malocclusion can be inherited, for example, or it can be caused by trauma, infection, or improper diet (such as if the hamster does not regularly eat foods hard enough to wear down his teeth). Even if you inspected your hamster's teeth before purchasing him, be aware that hereditary malocclusion is often not detectable in young hamsters. Even if the teeth appear normal at first, as the hamster grows, the teeth can become misaligned.

Disease Prevention

When properly cared for, hamsters are less stressed and have better natural resistance to diseases. For example, a clean cage is one of the most important ways you can help your hamster stay healthy, because spoiled food and a dirty cage are invitations to illness. Routine hygiene is the most effective way to prevent disease organisms from becoming established in your hamster's home and overpowering his natural resistance to disease. Your hamster is most likely to get sick when you become forgetful about cleaning his cage.

Pay attention to your pet's physical health and behavior. Note any weight changes, and feel for lumps and bumps. Significant changes in the amount of food or water consumed and in activity and behavior are also important to note and could signal illness. Knowing your hamster's regular behavior will better help you to detect when he is not feeling well.

Hamsters with this condition eventually cannot eat, lose weight, and will die without treatment. If you notice that your pet is not eating, you can check his incisors by pulling back his lips. Aside from the obvious misaligned or overgrown bite, hamsters can show a symptom often referred to as *slobbers*, which are threads of saliva around the mouth and sometimes wiped on the front paws.

Overgrown incisors are easily treated by a veterinarian. When the hamster is awake, the vet can clip the overgrown teeth. However, this procedure sometimes does not produce good long-term results and can cause other problems to develop. An incisor can split, fracture, or have jagged edges. If the tooth splinters all the way to the gum, it not only will cause the hamster pain, but it might also allow bacteria to enter the tooth and cause an abscess in the tooth's root. When clipped teeth are left with

Overgrown incisors are easily treated by a veterinarian.

jagged edges, the inside of the hamster's mouth and his tongue might be cut by the rough edges, causing discomfort and possible sites for infection. To prevent such problems, many veterinarians prefer to use a high-speed drill. The drill leaves a smooth surface while cutting through the overgrown incisors without splitting or fracturing them.

Improper Husbandry

When properly cared for, hamsters are less stressed and have better natural resistance to diseases. However, a plethora of problems can affect hamsters due to poor husbandry. The word "husbandry" describes how a pet is taken care of and includes aspects such as housing, food, and water.

Malocclusion occurs when a hamster's incisor teeth do not meet properly.

A hamster depends on you completely you to provide him with the proper environment. These animals cannot modify the size, temperature, air circulation, and cleanliness of their home. Providing a spacious, clean cage is one of the most important ways you can help your hamsters stay healthy. Because spoiled food and a dirty cage are invitations for illness, routine cleaning is the most effective method to prevent disease organisms from becoming established in your hamster's home and overpowering his natural resistance to disease. Your hamster is most likely to get sick when you become forgetful about cleaning his cage. Hamsters

Taking proper care of a sick hamster can help his recovery. Keep your sick pet in a warm, quiet area, and monitor his water and food intake. Inform your veterinarian if your hamster is constipated or has diarrhea. Carefully administer any medications that your veterinarian prescribes, and do not attempt to treat your pet with human medications or antibiotics bought at a pet store. Many of these medications are poisonous to hamsters and will kill your pet.

During treatment, it might be necessary to quarantine a sick hamster from any other hamsters you have, especially if the ailment is contagious or your sick pet needs undisturbed rest. Your veterinarian will let you know whether this is required.

After any kind of surgery, make sure that your hamster's cage remains clean to prevent any secondary bacterial infections of the surgery site. Check the incision site each day for swelling or discharge. Also, monitor whether your hamster is chewing the stitches. Be sure to consult with your veterinarian if your pet has not eaten or defecated within 24 hours after returning home.

often seem to tolerate a dirty environment. This trait is beneficial, since they are primarily children's pets and often suffer from occasional neglect. However, although they are hardy creatures, their tolerance can eventually diminish, and they will become ill if kept in an unsanitary environment. So keep your hamsters's cage, food and water bowl clean and you'll avoid many problems.

Senior Care

Hamsters are considered middle-aged when they are between 15 to 18 months of age, and a hamster who is 2 years old is considered to be a senior hamster. Senior hamsters are more prone to illnesses than when they were young. In fact, as your hamster gets older, you might begin to notice changes in his behavior and body condition due to aging. Besides

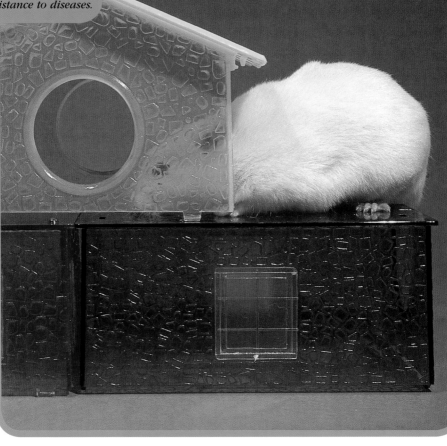

When properly cared for, hamsters are less stressed and have better natural resistance to diseases.

decreased activity naturally due to age, older hamsters move more slowly and can become inactive due to painful joints. Some old hamsters develop cataracts, which make their eyes appear milky. An animal with cataracts will eventually be unable to see, but he can still live a fulfilling life, and no treatment is necessary.

Many older hamsters lose weight due to undiagnosed (and untreatable) kidney diseases. If you notice that your hamster is eating less, check his incisors to be sure they still meet properly. Some experts think that older hamsters' teeth become fragile, so they are less able to eat hard foods. If you suspect that this is the case

Saying Goodbye

Most hamsters die in their sleep from old age or some undetected medical condition. However, in some cases, it might be better for a very old or very sick hamster to be painlessly put to sleep. Considering whether to euthanize a pet can be difficult, but your veterinarian can help you with this decision. For children, the loss of their hamster might be their first experience with death. Allowing a child to bury her hamster in a shoebox in the backyard can help her to say goodbye.

with your pet, try offering soft cooked foods such as cereals, rice, and pasta.

The fur of older hamsters begins to thin and may become patchy, with bald areas. Because of their thinning fur, be sure to provide your hamsters with plenty of warm nesting material. Older hamsters may also have a harder time grooming themselves and can be more susceptible to skin problems. You might need to assist by brushing them occasionally. The nails of older hamsters should also be routinely inspected in case they no longer keep them trim.

With proper maintenence a good diet, and plenty of loving care, your hamster should remain healthy throughout his life.

Older hamsters may have a harder time grooming themselves.

Chapter 6

Being Good

The fun part of owning a hamster is having him sit on your hand to eat a treat, taking him out of his cage to play, and watching him when runs on his wheel. This chapter will help you learn how to train your pet by winning his confidence and becoming his trusted friend.

Taming

The time you spend holding and playing with your hamster will help your pet learn to trust you and become tame. In fact, a tame hamster will let you hold him and pick him up without becoming frightened.

If your hamster is sleeping when you want to play with him, call his name, tap on his nest box, and allow

him several minutes to wake up before you visit. If you wake up your pet from a deep sleep, he will exhibit threatening behavior, such as rolling over on his back, baring his teeth, and perhaps growling and squawking. Do not persist, or you will get bitten. If you startle or grab your pet, you might also get bitten. Don't force your pet to come out of his nest box when he would clearly rather sleep. To avoid this problem, simply begin your taming sessions in the early evening, when your hamster is naturally awake. Establishing a routine, such as visiting with your hamster at the same time each evening, can help with the taming process.

Some hamsters are very wiggly and active. If your pet exhibits such behavior, it is best to start taming him by keeping your hand inside his cage, rather than taking him out of his enclosure. The following steps will help you to tame your pet:

Allow your hamster several minutes to wake up before you visit.

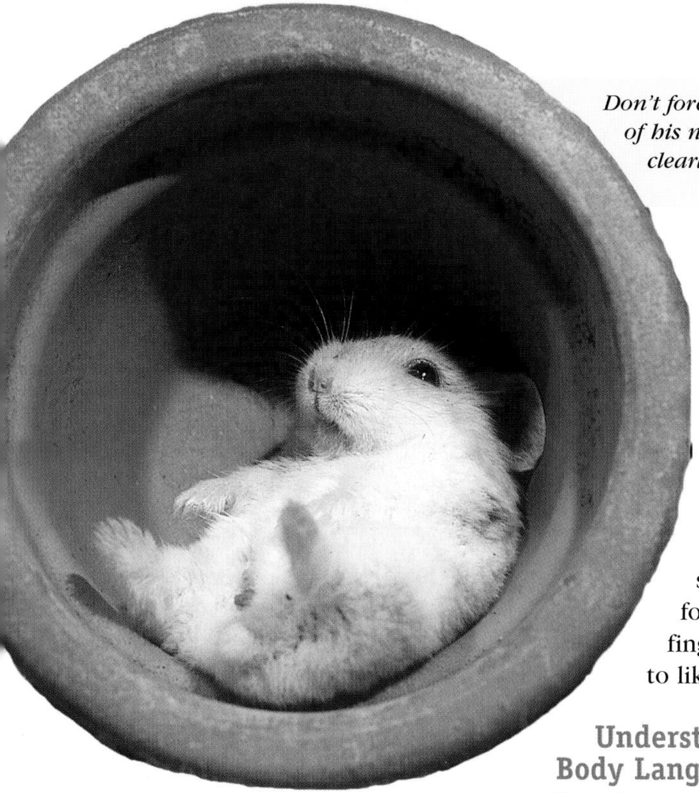

Expect the taming process to take several weeks. Some timid or nippy individuals take more time and patience. You can help earn your hamster's trust by remembering that the way to his heart is through his stomach. Offering some food or a tasty treat in your fingers will help him learn to like you.

95

Understanding Hamster Body Language

Knowing your hamster's body language can help you become more sensitive to your pet's moods and help you to tame him better.

You do not want to continue playing with your hamster if he becomes scared. You will be able to tell if he is frightened or nervous, for example, if he washes his face. As part of the "flight or fight response," some frightened hamsters might defecate or urinate. When frightened, your pet may also flatten himself close to the ground, run away, or bite. If your hamster engages in any of these behaviors, you should talk gently to him and then put him back into his house so that he can calm down.

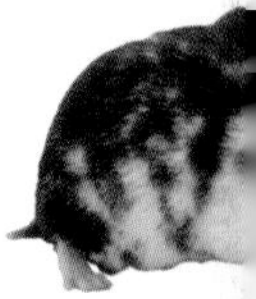

1. First, allow your hamster to sniff and crawl on your hand. Place a food treat in the palm of your hand, and encourage him to climb onto your hand. Do not make rapid movements with your hands.

2. If your hamster seems confident, try using a finger to pet him along his side or behind his ear. Even a brief stroke will work.

3. Continue to slowly pet your hamster within his cage while talking softly to him so that he becomes used to your voice.

Being Good

During both play and when they fight, the social dwarf hamsters often push at each other with their front paws. You might also hear your pets squeak or softly grind their teeth together when they are angry and ready to fight. A submissive hamster will try to appease a more dominant animal by walking stiffly away with his tail up. Fights among hamsters can be vicious, with the combatants inflicting serious bite wounds on each other. Among Syrian hamsters, fights can even lead to the death of one animal. Fighting hamsters typically lay their ears back, growl, and box with their front paws at each other. If one hamster does not flee, they will soon latch onto each other, rolling about as they fight. Fights often happen at night when pet owners are asleep. However, if you are around when your hamsters begin to fight, use a towel to separate them. Never use your hands, because you are likely to be accidentally bitten.

Some happy hamsters spring and leap in the air. Curious hamsters will stand up on their hind legs with ears alert and noses twitching to investigate their surroundings.

Holding Your Hamster

You can use one or both of the following methods to pick up your hamster: (1) use a container to scoop up your hamster, or (2) once he is tame, pick up your hamster by scooping him into both of your hands.

Once he is tame, you can pick up your hamster by scooping him in your hands.

Tricks for Kids

Some hamsters can be taught simple tricks such as sitting up on their hind legs for a treat or navigating through a homemade maze to get a treat. All tricks rely on a small piece of tasty food to reward the hamster. Because these animals are not generally as smart as other small pets such as rats, rabbits, and ferrets, it is easiest to train a behavior that they would normally do anyway, such as standing up on their hind legs, which they do to smell something interesting.

When training your hamster, you will start by rewarding him for exhibiting the desired behavior for a short period of time. Suppose you want to teach your hamster to stand and walk a few steps on his hind legs. You will start by rewarding your hamster when he merely stands up on his hind legs. Hold the food reward where your hamster can see or smell it when he is on all four legs, and then move the reward above his head so that he has to stand up to get it. You can also say, "Up" to your hamster at the same time. Eventually, you will want your pet to stay on his hind legs for longer periods of time before you reward him. Continue this method by moving the reward a little bit in front of him so that he has to walk to reach the reward. You can gradually extend the distance he has to walk on his hind legs until he has taken a few steps.

This type of training is called the method of approximation, or shaping. You can shape your hamster's behavior by rewarding those behaviors that are close to the behavior you want. As you train, have your hamster do a little more each time until he is behaving exactly as you want. You should use a food reward to reinforce your hamster's behavior. The food must be very tasty, and you should use only a very small piece, or your hamster will quickly fill up and lose interest in your training.

Using a Container

For dwarf hamsters, the cardboard roll from toilet paper will work as a scoop. Many dwarfs seem to enjoy the dark, burrow-like cardboard roll, but be sure to block both openings of the roll with your hands so that your pet won't accidentally leap out. Once your pet is tame, you can block only one end of the roll and pet your hamster when he peeks his head out at the other end.

For Syrian hamsters, a small, lightweight cardboard box or a tall cottage cheese container are good choices with which to pick up your pet. Hamsters do not like being scooped up in a plastic or glass container, because the smooth sides do not allow the animal to hold onto anything. Scooping up some shavings from the cage, along with your hamster, will make him less nervous when in a smooth, bare container.

Be sure that the container you choose will easily fit into and out of the cage. Do not chase your hamster around the cage with the container. Instead, place it on the cage floor near a corner, and gently coax and herd your hamster into it. You can also place a tasty treat inside the container to encourage your pet to willingly enter. Cover the top with one hand to prevent your hamster

Hamsters do not like to be held for very long or to be restrained while being held.

Rather than allow your hamster to explore the house, think of yourself as your pet's playground.

from leaping out. At the same time, talk reassuringly to him to help him learn that this procedure is nothing to fear.

Using Your Hands

Once your hamster is familiar with you and your hands, you can pick him up by letting him climb onto your hand or by scooping him up under his belly. Hamsters can be frightened when a hand descends over their back, so always put your hand in the cage palm up, lower it to the bottom of the cage, and then move it toward your pet.

Hamsters do not like to be held for very long or to be restrained while being held. If you try to hold your pet snugly in your hands, he will usually struggle and push through your fingers with his nose to try to get away. He might also try to bite you. Keep in mind that a normally docile hamster

might bite you when he is frightened. Before taking your pet out of his cage, it is important that you practice holding your hamster in his cage. That way, if he does bite you, you will not accidentally fling him to the ground.

Use one hand to hold your hamster, and lightly cup your other hand over his back or in front of his face. Use one of your hands to block or control his movements. With especially active dwarf hamsters, you will probably have to continually walk your hamster between your hands. Keep him close to your body for greater security. It is also prudent to immediately sit on the ground when holding your pet. Then, if he does jump, the distance is much less than if you were standing.

Hamsters are nimble, especially dwarfs. Even after your pet is calm and tame, always use two hands to hold him. Loud noises and sudden movements (your own or those caused by another person or pet) could scare your hamster and cause him to jump out of your hands. Hamsters can also take unpredictable leaps from your hand, so you need to be very careful.

Veterinarians often pick up a hamster using the loose skin on the back of his neck. Doing so reduces the animal's struggles and allows the vet to easily examine him. However, there really should be no reason for you to use this method. In addition, unless you pick him up by his skin just right, your hamster can rotate around inside his skin and bite you.

Playtime

Hamsters are fun to watch while they play in their cage. However, most pet owners want to take their hamsters out of their cage to play and explore. While other types of pets, such as rats, rabbits, and gerbils, can be allowed

to safely explore and play in a "pet-proofed" room (with "edible" items are removed from the floor, electrical cords safely placed away, and nooks and crannies closed up), hamsters are too small for such an activity. In particular, dwarf hamsters are so small that they can squeeze into spaces that you are unlikely to notice until it is too late. In short, the chance of your pet escaping and becoming lost are too great to allow him free rein. Moreover, hamsters are very difficult to recapture. Unlike other types of pets, if a hamster disappears from sight, he will tend to hide rather than becoming playfully interactive with his owner.

Rather than allow your hamster to explore the house, think of yourself as your pet's playground. Let him play on you while you sit on a bed or a chair. Whatever you do, never leave your pet unsupervised. Hamsters can quickly disappear into small nooks

Dwarf hamsters are territorial and usually do not accept an unfamiliar hamster.

An important caution about introducing a new hamster to your current pet is the potential risk of also introducing an illness. Serious hobbyists who breed hamsters usually quarantine a new arrival from their other hamsters, even if the newcomer seems healthy. A quarantine period helps prevent the transmission of illness among hamsters.

Quarantining an animal means that the new arrival is kept in a cage as far away as possible from the other animals. The quarantine period can last from 2 to 4 weeks. During this time, the new hamster's health is monitored. When the isolation period is over, the newcomer can be moved into the area containing the other hamsters, assuming he has exhibited no signs of ill health.

Pet owners rarely quarantine a new arrival, often because it means having to buy another cage and accessories. However, the best approach is to always quarantine a new arrival. If you purchased your new hamster from a serious breeder or a clean pet store, there is probably a low risk of any illness. Nonetheless, it is still a stressful time for both hamsters, and stress can cause hamsters to get sick.

Introduce new hamsters by placing their cages next to each other.

and crannies and be very hard to find. Hamsters also have no awareness of heights and will walk right off the edge of a bed, table, or chair, falling and potentially breaking a bone.

Other options for play outside your pet's cage include a bathroom tub, large plastic enclosures made especially for small pets that you can set up much like a child's playpen, or a high-sided plastic swimming pool. Place nest boxes and toys in the playground. Make sure that all these enclosures are escape proof.

Introducing Dwarf Hamsters to Each Other

Dwarf hamsters are territorial and usually do not accept an unfamiliar hamster. In fact, adult hamsters placed together in a cage for the first time will fight, sometimes until the death.

The purchase of a new cage is a cost that you should consider when buying a new hamster friend for your original pet. It is very important that the cage or cages you use for the introduction be new. Also, keep in mind that your original hamster will resent any newcomer's intrusion into his territory; he will aggressively defend his home, and the chances of a successful introduction will be reduced. Because of this, you should buy a younger hamster to increase the chances for success. Younger hamsters tend to be more readily accepted than another adult.

If one of your dwarf hamsters passes away, and you want to get your remaining hamster a companion, you must follow the steps described in this section.

Do not expect your hamster to get along with any other pets you may have. Even a parrot with clipped wings might leave his perch and dive-bomb an exploring hamster, if given the chance. As long as they can escape, hamsters can survive an encounter with more placid herbivorous pets such as guinea pigs and other hamsters, but an omnivorous pet rat will readily kill an unsupervised hamster.

Ferrets, cats, and dogs are a hamster's natural enemies. Your pet will not become friends with pets who are likely to kill and eat him. In fact, hamsters are the perfect size prey for cats, and few felines can resist stalking and pouncing on a hamster. Some people with obedience-trained dogs have taught them to let their hamsters smell and walk on them. Such dogs are unusual and typically have a low prey drive. Interestingly, the hamster will often behave aggressively toward the dog at first, nipping his feet or nose. But without any aggression from the dog, the hamster will eventually treat the dog as a play toy to run over and investigate.

While your other family pets will not be friends with your hamster, you must train them to leave him and his cage alone. Correct your dog if he barks, paws at the cage, jumps around, or otherwise scares your hamster. Do not let your cat sit on or lie down next to your hamster's cage. Boisterous dogs and persistent cats can knock over his cage, which is quite stressful and frightening for your tiny pet. If necessary, your hamster's home should be kept behind a closed door to protect him from other pets.

Hamsters are rodents, and they will chew on almost anything when given the chance.

Facilitating the Introduction

Several methods can be used to facilitate the introduction. First, place your original hamster in a wire cage, and place the new hamster in another wire cage. Slide the two cages together so that the hamsters can smell each other through the cage bars. Alternatively, you can try dividing a wire cage or aquarium with a piece of heavy gauge wire mesh. You must be certain to securely place the wire so that the weight of a hamster pressing against it will not cause the mesh to fall. If the mesh gives way, the

hamsters could reach each other, and they will fight. The spaces between the wire mesh should also be small enough that a hamster cannot push his nose through and bite the other hamster.

Over the next several days, switch the hamsters several times a day between the cages or sides of the cage. Usually the two animals will accept each other within several days, and you will be able to put them together. If they fight, you must continue switching them back and forth for several more days before once again housing them within the same cage.

Carefully watch your hamsters for the first few days that they share a home to make sure that they do not fight and have accepted one another. Any wounds from bites could indicate that the two hamsters still do not like each other. Providing two nesting boxes for your hamsters can reduce the likelihood of fighting.

Problems With Pairs

Sometimes a pair of hamsters that has been housed together for a long time might suddenly begin to fight.

It's also possible you never noticed the dynamics between the hamsters. If one of them is constantly chased, squeaks excessively, or hides by himself while the other hamster is out eating or playing, a problem could exist. Check to see if the timid hamster has chewed fur, especially near his rump, which is a sign that he has been bitten by the other hamster. More obvious signs of injury include torn ears or a missing tail. Providing a larger cage with two exercise wheels, two nest boxes, and two food dishes can reduce some of the conflict. However, if the less dominant hamster continues to be picked on, you will need to keep your hamsters in two separate cages.

Problem Behaviors

Hamsters do not have many problem behaviors. However, a few of the most common—back flipping and pacing, biting, and chewing—are described below.

Back Flipping and Pacing

Some Campbell's hamsters are born with behavioral abnormalities such as back flipping and pacing. These are genetic disorders that cannot be cured. Responsible breeders will not breed hamsters with these behaviors. If your hamster is affected with these traits, you should alert the breeder or pet store where you purchased your hamster. In some cases, hamsters with these behaviors can still make good pets.

Biting

The main hamster problem behavior is their tendency to bite when startled out of their sleep. Even tame hamsters retain their tendency to bite when tartled out of their sleep. This potential problem is easily prevented by respecting your hamster's need for uninterrupted rest. Do not disturb your sleeping hamster until he wakes up to play, or else first call his name and allow him to stretch, yawn, and slowly wake up. If he curls right back up into a sleeping ball, wait until later to visit with him.

Chewing

Hamsters are rodents, and they will chew on almost anything when given a chance. However, because your hamster will only be allowed to play outside his cage in a safe enclosure, he will have few opportunities to gnaw on books, clothes, furniture, or other valuable items. By closely supervising your pet, you can ensure his safety, as well as the well-being of your possessions.

Taming and training your hamster can take some time and dedication, but the end result is well worth it!

Resources

Clubs and Societies

American Hamster Association
www.afrma.org

American Rat, Mouse, and Hamster Society
8475 Westmore Road #30
San Diego, CA 92126
Telephone: (619) 390-2903
Fax: (619) 390-5271
www.altpet.net/rodents/rats/ARMHS.html

The British Hamster Association (BHA)
P.O. Box 825
Sheffield S17 3RU, UK
www.britishhamsterassociation.org.uk

The Hamster Society
www.hamsoc.org.uk

National Hamster Council (NHC)
National Secretary
P.O. Box 4
Llandovery
SA20 OZH
UK
E-mail: info@hamsters-uk.org
www.hamsters-uk.org

Rat, Mouse, and Hamster Fanciers
Membership
Sylvia Butler
RMHF Treasurer
188 School Street
Danville, CA 94526
www.ratmousehamster.com

Emergency services

ASPCA Animal Poison Control Center
1717 South Philo Road, Suite 36
Urbana, IL 61802
Telephone: (888) 426-4435
www.aspca.org

North Shore Animal League American and PROSAR
International Animal Poison Hotline
Telephone: (888) 232-8870
www.vetmedicine.about.com

Rescue Organizations

American Humane Association (AHA)
63 Inverness Drive East
Englewood, CO 80112
Telephone: (303) 792-9900
Fax: 792-5333
www.americanhumane.org

American Society for the Prevention of Cruelty to Animals (ASPCA)
424 E. 92nd Street
New York, NY 10128-6804
Telephone: (212) 876-7700
www.aspca.org

Royal Society for the Prevention of Cruelty to Animals (RSPCA)
Telephone: 0870 3335 999
Fax: 0870 7530 284
www.rspca.org.uk

The Humane Society of the United States (HSUS)
2100 L Street, NW
Washington DC 20037

Telephone: (202) 452-1100
www.hsus.org

Veterinary and Health Resources

Academy of Veterinary Homeopathy
(AVH)
P.O. Box 9280
Wilmington, DE 19809
Telephone: (866) 652-1590
Fax: (866) 652-1590
E-mail: office@TheAVH.org
www.theavh.org

American Academy of Veterinary
Acupuncture (AAVA)
100 Roscommon Drive, Suite 320
Middletown, CT 06457
Telephone: (860) 635-6300
Fax: (860) 635-6400
E-mail: office@aava.org
www.aava.org

American Animal Hospital Association
(AAHA)
P.O. Box 150899
Denver, CO 80215-0899
Telephone: (303) 986-2800
Fax: (303) 986-1700
E-mail: info@aahanet.org
www.aahanet.org/index.cfm

American College of Veterinary
Internal Medicine (ACVIM)
1997 Wadsworth Blvd., Suite A
Lakewood, CO 80214-5293
Telephone: (800) 245-9081
Fax: (303) 231-0880
Email: ACVIM@ACVIM.org
www.acvim.org

American College of Veterinary
Ophthalmologists (ACVO)
P.O. Box 1311
Meridian, Idaho 83860
Telephone: (208) 466-7624
Fax: (208) 466-7693
E-mail: office@acvo.com
www.acvo.com

American Holistic Veterinary Medical
Association (AHVMA)
2218 Old Emmorton Road
Bel Air, MD 21015
Telephone: (410) 569-0795
Fax: (410) 569-2346
E-mail: office@ahvma.org
www.ahvma.org

American Veterinary Medical
Association (AVMA)
1931 North Meacham Road – Suite 100
Schaumburg, IL 60173
Telephone: (847) 925-8070
Fax: (847) 925-1329
E-mail: avmainfo@avma.org
www.avma.org

ASPCA Animal Poison Control Center
1717 South Philo Road, Suite 36
Urbana, IL 61802
Telephone: (888) 426-4435
www.aspca.org

British Veterinary Association (BVA)
7 Mansfield Street
London
W1G 9NQ
Telephone: 020 7636 6541
Fax: 020 7436 2970
E-mail: bvahq@bva.co.uk
www.bva.co.uk

Orthopedic Foundation for Animals
(OFA)
2300 NE Nifong Blvd
Columbus, Missouri 65201-3856
Telephone: (573) 442-0418
Fax: (573) 875-5073
Email: ofa.offa.org
www.offa.org

Publications

Barrie, Anmarie. *Hamsters as a New Pet.* Neptune City: T.F.H. Publications, Inc., 2002.

Barrie, Anmarie. *The Guide to Owning a Hamster.* Neptune City: T.F.H. Publications, Inc., 2003.

Logsdail, Chris, et al. *Hamsterlopaedia: A Complete Guide to Hamster Care.* Ringpress Books, 2004.

T.F.H. Staff Experts. *Quick & Easy Hamster Care.* Neptune City: T.F.H. Publications, Inc., 2002.

Vanderslip, Sharon L., DVM. *Dwarf Hamsters: A Complete Pet Owner's Manual.* Barron's Educational Series, 1999.

von Frisch, Otto. *Hamsters: A Complete Pet Owner's Manual.* Barron's Educational Series, 1998.

Internet Resources

www.1888pets911.org
Pets 911offers a comprehensive database of lost and found pets, adoption information, pet health, and shelter and rescue information. The website also runs a toll-free telephone hotline (1-888-PETS-911) that gives pet owners access to important life-saving information.

www.healthypet.com
Healthypet.com is part of the American Animal Hospital Association (AAHA), an organization of more than 29,000 veterinary care providers committed to providing excellence in small animal care.

www.petfinder.org
Petfinder.org provides an extensive database of adoptable animals, shelters, and rescue groups around the country. You can also post classified ads for lost or found pets, pets wanted, and pets needing homes.

Hamsters

Index

Index

Hamsters

111

Index

About the Author
Sue Fox is the author of numerous books on small animals and several breeds of dog. Her home in the Sierra Nevada Mountains of California is shared with a happy menagerie.

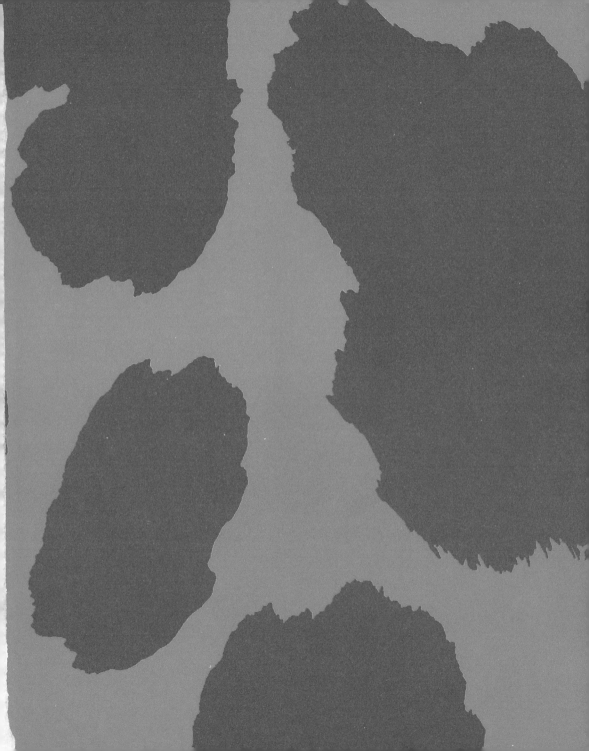